Lyra Apostolica

John Keble, John Henry Newman, Robert Isaac Wilberforce, John William Bowden, Richard Hurrell Froude, Isaac Williams

BIBLIOLIFE

LYRA
APOSTOLICA.

Γνοῖεν δ', ὡς δὴ δῆρον ἐγὼ πολέμοιο πέπαυμαι.

SIXTH EDITION.

DERBY:
HENRY MOZLEY AND SONS;
PARKER, OXFORD; AND J. G. & F. RIVINGTON,
ST. PAUL'S CHURCH YARD, AND WATERLOO PLACE, LONDON.
1843.

ADVERTISEMENT.

THE following compositions have been reprinted from the British Magazine, where they had the advantage of originally appearing, in the humble hope that they may be instrumental in recalling or recommending to the reader important Christian truths which are at this day in a way to be forgotten. The publication, having no other object but this, would, according to the original intention, have been strictly anonymous, but one of the writers, in whom the work originated, having been taken from his friends by death, it seemed desirable so far to depart from it, as to record what belonged to him, while it was possible to do so; and this has led to a general discrimination of the poems by signatures at the end of each.

OXFORD,
The Feast of all Saints, 1836.

CONTENTS.

CONTENTS.

CONTENTS.

CONTENTS.

CONTENTS.

CONTENTS.

CONTENTS.

LYRA APOSTOLICA.

HOME.

I.

WHERE'ER I roam in this fair English land,
  The vision of a temple meets my eyes:
  Modest without; within, all glorious rise
Its love en-clustered columns, and expand
Their slender arms. Like olive-plants they stand,
  Each answering each, in home's soft sympathies,
  Sisters·and brothers   At the Altar sighs
Parental fondness, and with anxious hand
Tenders its offering of young vows and prayers.
The same and not the same, go where I will,
The vision beams! ten thousand shrines, all one.
Dear fertile soil! what foreign culture bears
Such fruit? And I through distant climes may run
My weary round, yet miss thy likeness still.

δ.

II.

Ere yet I left home's youthful shrine,
　My heart and hope were stored
Where first I caught the rays divine,
　And drank the Eternal Word.

I went afar; the world unrolled
　Her many-pictured page;
I stored the marvels which she told,
　And trusted to her gage.

Her pleasures quaff'd, I sought awhile
　The scenes I prized before:
But parent's praise and sister's smile
　Stirred my cold heart no more.

So ever sear, so ever cloy
　Earth's favours as they fade,
Since Adam lost for one fierce joy
　His Eden's sacred shade.

　　　　　　　　　　　　　　　δ.

III.

My home is now a thousand mile away ;
   Yet in my thoughts its every image fair
   Rises as keen, as I still lingered there,
And, turning me, could all I loved survey.
And so upon Death's unaverted day,
   As I speed upward, I shall on me bear,
   And in no breathless whirl, the things that were,
And duties given, and ends I did obey.
And, when at length I reach the Throne of Power,
Ah ! still unscared, I shall in fulness see
The vision of my past innumerous deeds,
My deep heart-courses, and their motive-seeds,
So to gaze on till the red dooming hour.
Lord ! in that strait, the Judge ! remember me !

                                 δ.

Home.

How can I keep my Christmas feast
  In its due festive show,
Reft of the sight of the High Priest
  From whom its glories flow?

I hear the tuneful bells around,
  The blessed towers I see;
A stranger on a foreign ground,
  They peal a fast for me.

O Britons! now so brave and high,
  How will ye weep the day
When CHRIST in judgment passes by,
  And calls the Bride away!

Your Christmas then will lose its mirth,
  Your Easter lose its bloom:—
Abroad, a scene of strife and dearth;
  Within, a cheerless home!

                                    δ.

v.

BANISHED the House of sacred rest,
   Amid a thoughtless throng,
At length I heard its Creed confessed,
   And knelt the Saints among.

Artless his strain and unadorned,
   Who spoke CHRIST's message there;
But what at home I might have scorned,
   Now charmed my famished ear.

LORD, grant me this abiding grace,
   Thy Word and Sons to know;
To pierce the veil on Moses' face,
   Although his speech be slow!

ε.

REMORSE.

VI.

SHAME.

I BEAR upon my brow the sign
  Of sorrow and of pain :
Alas! no hopeful cross is mine,
  It is the mark of Cain.

The course of passion, and the fret
  Of godless hope and fear,—
Toil, care, and guilt,—their hues have set,
  And fixed that sternness there.

Saviour! wash out the imprinted shame ;
  That I no more may pine,
Sin's martyr, though not meet to claim
  Thy cross, a saint of Thine.

ĉ.

VII.

BONDAGE.

Oh, prophet, tell me not of peace,
　Or Christ's all-loving deeds ;
Death only can from sin release,
　And death to judgment leads.

Thou from thy birth hast set thy face
　Towards thy Redeemer Lord ;
To tend and deck his holy place,
　And note His secret word.

I ne'er shall reach Heaven's glorious path ;
　Yet haply tears may stay
The purpose of His instant wrath,
　And slake the fiery day.

Then plead for me, thou blessed saint,
　While I in haste begin
All man e'er guessed of work or plaint
　To wash away my sin.

δ.

VIII.

TERROR.

O FATHER, list a sinner's call!
Fain would I hide from man my fall—
  But I must speak, or faint—
I cannot wear guilt's silent thrall.
  Cleanse me, kind Saint!

" Sinner ne'er blunted yet sin's goad;
Speed thee, my son, a safer road,
  And sue His pardoning smile
Who walked woe's depths, bearing man's load
  Of guilt the while."

Yet raise a mitigating hand,
And minister some potion bland,
  Some present fever-stay!
Lest one for whom His work was planned
  Die of dismay.

" Peace cannot be, hope must be thine ;
I can but lift the Mercy-sign.

This wouldst thou ? It shall be '
Kneel down, and take the word divine,
ABSOLVO TE."

 δ.

IX.

RESTLESSNESS

ONCE, as I brooded o'er my guilty state,
A fever seiz'd me, duties to devise
To buy my interest in my Saviour's eyes ﹕
Not that His love I would extenuate,
But scourge and penance, and perverse self-hate,
Or gift of cost, served by an artifice
To quell my restless thoughts and envious sighs
And doubts, which fain heaven's peace would antedate.
Thus, as I tossed, He said :—" Even holiest deeds
Shroud not the soul from God, nor soothe its needs ;
Deny thee thine own fears, and wait the end !"
Stern lesson ! Let me con it day by day,
And learn to kneel before the Omniscient Ray,
Nor shrink, while Truth's avenging shafts descend !

δ.

THE PAST AND THE PRESENT.

X.

THE PAINS OF MEMORY.

WHAT time my heart unfolded its fresh leaves
  In springtime gay, and scatter'd flowers around,
  A whisper warned of earth's unhealthy ground,
And all that there faith's light and pureness grieves ;
    Sun's ray and canker-worm,
    And sudden-whelming storm ;—
But, ah ! my self-will smiled, nor recked the gracious
    sound

So now defilement dims life's morning springs ;
  I cannot hear an early-cherished strain,
  But first a joy, and then it brings a pain—
Fear, and self-hate, and vain remorseful stings :
    Tears lull my grief to rest,
    Not without hope, this breast
May one day lose its load, and youth yet bloom again
                    δ.

XI.

DREAMS.

OH ! miserable power
To dreams allowed, to raise the guilty past,
And back awhile the illumined spirit to cast
   On its youth's twilight hour ;—
In mockery guiling it to act again
The revel or the scoff in Satan's frantic train !

   Nay, hush thee, angry heart !
An Angel's grief ill fits a penitent ;
Welcome the thorn—it is divinely sent,
   And with its wholesome smart
Shall pierce thee in thy virtue's home serene,
And warn thee what thou art, and whence thy wealth
   has been.

                        δ.

XII.

CONFESSION.

My smile is bright, my glance is free,
  My voice is calm and clear;
Dear friend, I seem a type to thee
  Of holy love and fear.

But I am scanned by eyes unseen,
  And these no saint surround;
They mete what is by what has been,
  And joy the lost is found.

Erst my good Angel shrank to see
  My thoughts and ways of ill;
And now he scarce dare gaze on me,
  Scar-seamed and crippled still.

$\delta.$

XIII

AWE.

I bow at Jesus' Name, for 'tis the Sign
Of awful mercy towards a guilty line.—
Of shameful ancestry, in birth defiled,
    And upwards from a child
Full of unlovely thoughts and rebel aims
    As hastening judgment flames,
How can I lightly view my Means of life ?—
The Just assailing sin, and death-strained in the strife !

And so, albeit His woe is our release,
Thought of that woe aye dims our earthly peace ;
The Life is hidden in a Fount of Blood !—
    And this is tidings good,
But in the Angel's reckoning, and to those
    Who Angel-wise have chose
And kept, like Paul, a virgin course, content
    To go where Jesus went ;
But for the many laden with the spot
And earthly taint of sin, 'tis written, "'Touch Me not."

                      $\delta.$

XIV.

THE CROSS OF CHRIST.

" Ad omnem progressum atque promotum, ad omnem aditum et exitum, ad vestitum, ad calciatum, ad lavacra, ad mensas, ad lumina, ad cubilia, ad sedilia, quacunque nos conversatio exercet, frontem Crucis signaculo terimus." *Tertull. de Corona*, § 3.

WHENE'ER across this sinful flesh of mine
    I draw the Holy Sign,
All good thoughts stir within me, and collect
    Their slumbering strength divine ;
Till there springs up that hope of GOD's elect
    My faith shall ne'er be wrecked.

And who shall say, but hateful spirits around,
    For their brief hour unbound,
Shudder to see, and wail their overthrow ?
    While on far heathen ground
Some lonely Saint hails the fresh odour, though
    Its source he cannot know.

                              δ.

FORGIVENESS.

XV.

THE THREE ABSOLUTIONS *

" And there shall in nowise enter into it any thing that defileth,
neither whatsoever worketh abomination, or maketh a lie ; but
they which are written in the Lamb's Book of Life "

EACH morn and eve, the Golden Keys
    Are lifted in the sacred hand,
To shew the sinner on his knees
    Where heaven's bright doors wide open stand.

On the dread Altar duly laid
    The Golden Keys their witness bear,
That not in vain the Church hath pray'd,
    That He, the Life of Souls, is there.

* 1. In the Daily Service. 2. In the Communion. 3. In the
Visitation of the Sick.

Full of the past, all shuddering thought,
   Man waits his hour with upward eye—[*]
The Golden Keys in love are brought
   That he may hold by them and die.

But touch them trembling ; for that gold
   Proves iron in the unworthy hand,
To close, not ope, the favour'd fold,
   To bind, not loose, the lost soul's band.

                     7.

XVI.

" And the Spirit and the Bride say, Come. And let him that
heareth say, Come. And let him that is athirst come. And who-
soever will, let him take of the waters of life freely."

O LORD, I hear, but can it be
The gracious word was meant for me?
O Lord, I thirst, but who shall tell
The secret of that living well,
   By whose waters I may rest
   And slake this lip unblest ?

[*] Vid Death-bed Scenes, " The Barton Family." § 3.

O Lord, I will, but cannot do,
My heart is hard, my faith untrue ·
The Spirit and the Bride say, Come,
The eternal ever-blessed Home
  Ope'd its portals at my birth,
  But I am chained to earth :

The Golden Keys each eve and morn
I see them with a heart forlorn
Lest they should Iron prove to me —
O set my heart at liberty.
  May I seize what Thou dost give,
  Seize tremblingly and live.

                           β.

XVII.

" He which testifieth these things saith, Surely I come quickly."

FEAR NOT · for he hath sworn :
  Faithful and true His name :
The glorious hours are onward borne ;
  'Tis lit, th' immortal flame ;
It glows *around* thee ; kneel, and strive, and win
Daily one living ray—'twill brighter glow *within*.

YET FEAR : the time is brief ;
　The Holy One is near ;
And like a spent and withered leaf
　In autumn-twilight drear,
Faster each hour, on Time's unslackening gale,
The dreaming world drives on, to where all vision fail.

Surely the time is short :
　Endless the task and art
To brighten for the ethereal court
　A soil'd earth-drudging heart.—
But He, the dread Proclaimer of that hour,
Is pledged to thee in Love, as to thy foes in Power.

His shoulders bear the Key :
　He opens—who can close ?
Closes—and who dare open ?—He
　Thy soul's misgiving knows.
If He come quick, the mightier sure will prove
His Spirit in each heart that timely strives to love.

Then haste Thee, Lord ! Come down,
 Take Thy great Power, and reign !
But frame Thee first a perfect Crown
 Of spirits freed from stain,
Souls mortal once, now match'd for evermore,
With the immortal gems that form'd Thy wreath before

Who in Thy portal wait,
 Free of that glorious throng,
Wondering, review their trial-state,
 The life that erst seemed long ;
Wondering at His deep love, who purg'd so base
And earthly mould so soon for th' undefiled place.

       γ.

ΑΜΗΝ ΝΑΙ ΕΡΧΟΥ, ΚΥΡΙΕ ΙΗΣΟΥ

        β.

AFFLICTION.

XVIII.

DAVID AND JONATHAN.

" Thy love to me was wonderful, passing the love of women "

O HEART of fire ! misjudged by wilful man,
    Thou flower of Jesse's race !
What woe was thine, when thou and Jonathan
    Last greeted face to face !
He doom'd to die, thou on us to impress
The portent of a blood-stained holiness.

Yet it was well :—for so, mid cares of rule
    And crime's encircling tide,
A spell was o'er thee, zealous one, to cool
    Earth-joy and kingly pride ;
With battle-scene and pageant, prompt to blend
The pale calm spectre of a blameless friend.

Ah! had he lived, before thy throne to stand,
  Thy spirit keen and high,
Sure it had snapped in twain love's slender band,
  So dear in memory,
Paul's strife unblest,* its serious lesson gives,
He bides with us who dies, he is but lost who lives.

                                        δ.

XIX.

" Blessed be ye poor "

I HAVE been honoured and obeyed,
  I have met scorn and slight;
And my heart loves earth's sober shade
  More than her laughing light.

For what is rule but a sad weight
  Of duty and a snare?
What meanness, but with happier fate
  The SAVIOUR's Cross to share?

* Acts xv. 39.

'This my hid choice, though not from heaven,
  Moves on the heavenward line ;
Cleanse it, good Lord, from sinful leaven,
  And make it simply Thine.

δ.

XX.

MOSES.

Moses, the patriot fierce, became
  The meekest man on earth,
To shew us how love's quickening flame
  Can give our souls new birth.

Moses, the man of meekest heart,
  Lost Canaan by self-will,
To shew, where Grace has done its part,
  How sin defiles us still.

Thou, who hast taught me in Thy fear,
  Yet seest me frail at best,
O grant me loss with Moses here,
  To gain his future rest !

δ.

XXI

"And we indeed justly; for we receive the due reward of our
deeds."

MORTAL! if e'er thy spirits faint,
   By grief or pain opprest,
Seek not vain hope, or sour complaint,
   To cheer or ease thy breast;

But view thy bitterest pangs as sent
   A shadow of that doom,
Which is thy soul's just punishment
   In its own guilt's true home.

Be thine own judge : hate thy proud heart;
   And while the sad drops flow,
E'en let thy will attend the smart,
   And sanctify thy woe.

$\delta.$

XXII.

DAVID NUMBERING THE PEOPLE.

I am in a great strait—let me fall now into the hand of the Lord

If e'er I fall beneath Thy rod,
  As through life's snares I go,
Save me from David's lot, O God!
  And choose Thyself the woe.

How should I face Thy plagues? which scare,
  And haunt, and stun, until
The heart or sinks in mute despair,
  Or names a random ill.

If else . . . then guide in David's path,
  Who chose the holier pain ;
Satan and man are tools of wrath,
  An Angel's scourge is gain.

δ.

XXIII.

Thou in faithfulness hast afflicted me.

LORD, in this dust Thy sovereign voice
  First quickened love divine ;
I am all Thine,—Thy care and choice,
  My very praise is Thine.

I praise Thee, while Thy providence
  In childhood frail I trace,
For blessings given, ere dawning sense
  Could seek or scan Thy grace ;

Blessings in boyhood's marvelling hour,
  Bright dreams, and fancyings strange ;
Blessings, when reason's awful power
  Gave thought a bolder range ;

Blessings of friends, which to my door
  Unasked, unhoped, have come ;
And, choicer still, a countless store
  Of eager smiles at home.

Yet, Lord, in memory's fondest place
    I shrine those seasons sad,
When, looking up, I saw Thy face
    In kind austereness clad.

I would not miss one sigh or tear,
    Heart-pang, or throbbing brow;
Sweet was the chastisement severe,
    And sweet its memory now.

Yes! let the fragrant scars abide,
    Love-tokens in Thy stead,
Faint shadows of the spear-pierced side,
    And thorn-encompassed head.

And such Thy loving force be still,
    Mid life's fierce shifting fray,
Shaping to Truth self's froward will
    Along Thy narrow way.

Deny me wealth; far, far remove
    The lure of power or name,
Hope thrives in straits, in weakness Love,
    And faith in this world's shame.

δ.

FAITH.

XXIV.

ABRAHAM.

THE better portion didst thou choose, Great Heart,
  Thy GOD's first choice, and pledge of Gentile-
      grace !
  Faith's truest type, he with unruffled face
Bore the world's smile, and bade her slaves depart;
Whether, a trader, with no trader's art,
  He buys in Canaan his first resting-place,—
  Or freely yields rich Siddim's ample space,—
Or braves the rescue and the battle's smart,
Yet scorns the heathen gifts of those he saved.
O happy in their soul's high solitude,
Who commune thus with GOD and not with earth !
Amid the scoffings of the wealth-enslaved,
A ready prey, as though in absent mood
They calmly move, nor hear the unmannered mirth.

$\delta.$

XXV.

Unto the godly there ariseth up light in the darkness.

LEAD, Kindly Light, amid the encircling gloom,
　　Lead Thou me on !
The night is dark, and I am far from home—
　　Lead thou me on !
Keep Thou my feet ; I do not ask to see
The distant scene,—one step enough for me.

I was not ever thus, nor prayed that Thou
　　Shouldst lead me on.
I loved to choose and see my path ; but now,
　　Lead thou me on !
I loved the garish day, and, spite of fears,
Pride ruled my will : remember not past years.

So long Thy power hath blest me, sure it still
　　Will lead me on,
O'er moor and fen, o'er crag and torrent till
　　The night is gone ;

And with the morn those Angel faces smile
Which I have loved long since, and lost awhile.

δ.

XXVI.

"It is I: be not afraid."*

WHEN I sink down in gloom or fear,
   Hope blighted or delayed,
Thy whisper, Lord, my heart shall cheer,
   " 'Tis I; be not afraid !"

Or, startled at some sudden blow,
   If fretful thoughts I feel,
" Fear not, it is but I !" shall flow,
   As balm my wound to heal.

---

* Vid. Bishop Wilson's Sacra Privata for Friday. The above
lines were written before the appearance of Mr. Lyte's elegant
Poem on the same text.

Nor will I quit Thy way, though foes
   Some onward pass defend ;
From each rough voice the watchword goes,
   " Be not afraid ! . . . a friend !"

And O ! when judgment's trumpet clear
   Awakes me from the grave,
Still in its echo may I hear,
   " 'Tis Christ ! he comes to save."

                                    $\delta.$

XXVII.

The Lord stood with me and strengthened me

O SAY not thou art left of God,
   Because His tokens in the sky
Thou canst not read ; this earth He trod
   To teach thee He was ever nigh.

He sees, beneath the fig-tree green,
   Nathaniel con His sacred lore ;
Shouldst thou the closet seek, unseen
   He enters through the unopened door.

And, when thou liest, by slumber bound,
　Outwearied in the Christian fight,
In glory, girt with Saints around,
　He stands above thee through the night.

When friends to Emmaus bend their course,
　He joins, although He holds their eyes ;
Or, shouldst thou feel some fever's force,
　He takes thy hand, He bids thee rise.

Or, on a voyage, when calms prevail,
　And prison thee upon the sea,
He walks the wave, He wings the sail,
　The shore is gained, and thou art free.

　　　　　　　　　　　　　　δ.

XXVIII.

JAMES AND JOHN.

Two brothers freely cast their lot,
　With David's royal Son,
The cost of conquest counting not,
　They deem the battle won.

Brothers in heart, they hope to gain
   An undivided joy,
That man may one with man remain,
   As boy was one with boy.

Christ heard; and willed that James should fa
   First prey of Satan's rage;
John linger out his fellows all,
   And die in bloodless age.

Now they join hands once more above
   Before the Conqueror's throne;
Thus GOD grants prayer; but in His love
   Makes times and ways His own.

                                 δ.

XXIX.

"Whither I go, thou canst not follow Me now, but thou shalt follow Me afterwards."

Did we but see,
When life first opened, how our journey lay
Between its earliest and its closing day;
   Or view ourselves, as we one time shall be,
Who strive for the high prize, such sight would break
The youthful spirit, though bold for Jesus' sake.

   But Thou, dear Lord!
Whilst I traced out bright scenes which were to come,
Isaac's pure blessings, and a verdant home,
   Didst spare me, and withhold Thy fearful word;
Wiling me year by year, till I am found
A pilgrim pale, with Paul's sad girdle bound.

δ.

PROVIDENCES.

XXX.

GUARDIAN ANGELS.

ARE these the tracks of some unearthly Friend,
  His foot-prints, and his vesture-skirts of light,
  Who, as I talk with men, conforms aright
Their sympathetic words, or deeds that blend
With my hid thought;—or stoops him to attend
  My doubtful-pleading grief;—or blunts the might
  Of ill I see not;—or in dreams of night
Figures the scope in which what is will end?
Were I Christ's own, then fitly might I call
That vision real; for to the thoughtful mind
That walks with Him, He half unveils his face;
But when on common men such shadows fall,
These dare not make their own the gifts they find,
Yet, not all hopeless, eye His boundless grace.

δ.

XXXI.

WARNINGS.

(For Music.)

WHEN Heaven sends sorrow,
 Warnings go first,
 Lest it should burst
 With stunning might
 On souls too bright
  To fear the morrow.

Can science bear us
  To the hid springs
  Of human things ?
  Why may not dream,
  Or thought's day gleam,
   Startle, yet cheer us ?

Are such thoughts fetters,
  While faith disowns
  Dread of earth's tones,
  Recks but Heaven's call,
  And on the wall,
   Reads but Heaven's letters ?

       δ.

E

XXXII.

DISCIPLINE.

WHEN I look back upon my former race,
  Seasons I see, at which the Inward Ray,
  More brightly burned, or guided some new way;
Truth, in its wealthier scene and nobler space,
Given for my eye to range, and feet to trace,
  And next I mark, 'twas trial did convey,
  Or grief, or pain, or strange eventful day,
To my tormented soul such larger grace.
So now, whene'er, in journeying on, I feel
The shadow of the Providential Hand,
Deep breathless stirrings shoot across my breast,
Searching to know what He will now reveal,
What sin uncloak, what stricter rule command,
And girding me to work His full behest.

                                              δ.

LIFE IMMORTAL.

XXXIII.

Whene'er I seek the Holy Altar's rail,
  And kneel to take the grace there offered me,
It is no time to task my reason frail,
  To try Christ's words, and search how they may be ;
Enough, I eat His Flesh and drink His Blood,
More is not told—to ask it is not good.

I will not say with these, that bread and wine
  Have vanished at the consecration prayer ;
Far less with those deny that aught divine
  And of immortal seed is hidden there.
Hence, disputants ! The din, which ye admire,
Keeps but ill measure with the Church's choir.

δ.

XXXIV.

He is not the God of the dead, but of the living; for all live unto Him

" THE Fathers are in dust, yet live to God :"—
 So says the Truth; as if the motionless clay
Still held the seeds of life beneath the sod,
 Smouldering and struggling till the judgment-day.

And hence we learn with reverence to esteem
 Of these frail houses, though the grave confines;
Sophist may urge his cunning tests, and deem
 That they are earth;—but they are heavenly shrines.

δ.

HOLINESS.

XXXV.

DANIEL

εἰσιν εὐνοῦχοι, οἵτινες εὐνούχισαν ἑαυτοὺς διὰ τὴν βασιλείαν τῶν οὐρανῶν.

Son of sorrow, doom'd by fate
To a lot most desolate,
To joyless youth and childless age,
Last of thy father's lineage,
Blighted being! whence hast thou
That lofty mien and cloudless brow?

Ask'st thou whence that cloudless brow?
Bitter is the cup I trow;
A cup of weary well-spent years,
A cup of sorrows, fasts, and tears,
That cup whose virtue can impart
Such calmness to the troubled heart.

E 3

Last of his father's lineage, he
Many a night on bended knee,
In hunger many a livelong day,
Hath striven to cast his slough away.
Yea, and that long prayer is granted;
Yea, his soul is disenchanted.

O blest above the sons of men!
For thou with more than prophet's ken,
Deep in the secrets of the tomb,
Hast read thine own, thine endless doom.
Thou by the hand of the Most High
Art sealed for immortality.

So may I read thy story right,
And in my flesh so tame my spright,
That when the mighty ones go forth,
And from the east and from the north
Unwilling ghosts shall gathered be,
I in my lot* may stand with thee.

β.

---

* Dan. xii. 13.

XXXVI

" Be strong, and He shall comfort thine heart.'

" Lord, I have fasted, I have prayed,
  And sackcloth has my girdle been,
To purge my soul I have essayed
  With hunger blank and vigil keen.
O God of mercy! why am I
Still haunted by the self I fly ?"

Sackcloth is a girdle good,
  O bind it round thee still;
Fasting, it is Angel's food,
  And Jesus loved the night-air chill;
Yet think not prayer and fast were given
To make one step 'twixt earth and heaven.

β.

XXXVII

The effectual fervent prayer of a righteous man availeth much

THERE is not on the earth a soul so base
　　But may obtain a place
　　In covenanted grace ;
So that forthwith his prayer of faith obtains
　　Release of his guilt-stains,
And first-fruits of the second birth, which rise
From gift to gift, and reach at length the eternal prize.

All may save self,—but minds that heavenward tower
　　Aim at a wider power,
　　Gifts on the world to shower.—
And this is not at once ,—by fastings gained,
　　And trials well sustained,
By pureness, righteous deeds, and toils of love,
Abidance in the Truth, and zeal for God above.

$\delta.$

XXXVIII.

JOSEPH.

O PUREST semblance of the Eternal Son!
Who dwelt in thee as in some blessed shrine,
To draw hearts after thee and make them thine;
Not parent only by that light was won,
And brethren crouched who had in wrath begun,
E'en heathen pomp abased her at the sign
Of a hid God, and drank the sound divine,
Till a king heard, and all thou badst was done.
Then was fulfilled Nature's dim augury,
That, " Wisdom clad, in visible form, would be
So fair, that all must love and bow the knee ,"*
Lest it might seem, what time the Substance came,
Truth lacked a sceptre, when It but laid by
Its beaming front, and bore a willing shame.

δ.

---

* Η φρόνησις οὐχ ὁρᾶται· δεινοὺς γὰρ ἂν παρεῖχεν ἔρωτας, εἰ τοιοῦτον ἑαυτῆς ἐναργὲς εἴδωλον παρείχετο εἰς ὄψιν ἰόν.

PLAT. *Phæd.*

SOLITUDE.

XXXIX.

THE HAVEN.

Whence is this awe, by stillness spread
　　O'er the world-fretted soul?
Wave reared on wave its boastful head,
While my keen bark, by breezes sped,
Dash'd fiercely through the ocean bed,
　　And chafed towards its goal.

But now there reigns so deep a rest,
　　That I could almost weep.
Sinner! thou hast in this rare guest
Of Adam's peace a figure blest;
'Tis Eden seen, but not possessed,
　　Which cherub flames still keep.

δ.

XL.

THE DESERT.

Two sinners have been grace-endued
    Unwearied to sustain
For forty days a solitude
    On mount and desert plain.

But feverish thoughts the breasts have swayed,
    And gloom or pride is shown,
If e'er we seek the garden's shade,
    Or walk the world, alone.

For Adam e'en, before his sin,
    His God a help-meet found;
Blest with an Angel's heart within,
    Paul wrought with friends around.

Lone saints of old! of purpose high,
    On Syria's sands ye claim,
'Mid heathen rage, our sympathy,
    In peace ye force our blame.

δ.

XLI.

DEATH

Whene'er goes forth Thy dread command,
    And my last hour is nigh,
Lord, grant me in a Christian land,
    As I was born, to die.

I pray not, Lord, that friends may be
    Or kindred standing by ;
Choice blessing ! which I leave to Thee,
    To give me, or deny.

But let my failing limbs beneath
    My Mother's smile recline ,
My name in sickness and in death
    Heard in her sacred shrine.

And may the Cross beside my bed
    In its meet emblems rest ;
And may the absolving words be said
    To ease a laden breast.

Thou, Lord! where'er we lie, canst aid;
    But He, who taught His own
To live as one, will not upbraid
    The dread to die alone.

δ.

VANITY OF VANITIES.

XLII.

Man walketh in a vain shadow, and disquieteth himself in vain

THEY do but grope in learning's pedant round,
  Who on the fantasies of sense bestow
  An idol substance, bidding us bow low
Before those shades of being which are found
Stirring or still on man's brief trial ground;
  As if such shapes and moods, which come and g
  Had aught of Truth or Life in their poor show,
To sway or judge, and skill to sain or wound.
Son of immortal Seed, high destined Man!
Know thy dread gift,—a creature, yet a cause;
Each mind is its own centre, and it draws
Home to itself, and moulds in its thought's span,
All outward things, the vassals of its will,
Aided by Heaven, by earth unthwarted still.

δ.

XLIII.

Felix, qui potuit rerum cognoscere causas,
Atque metus omnes, et inexorabile fatum
Subjecit pedibus, strepitumque Acherontis avari [1]

In childhood, when with eager eyes
    The season-measured year I viewed,
        All, garbed in fairy guise,
           Pledged constancy of good.

Spring sang of heaven; the summer-flowers
    Let me gaze on, and did not fade;
        Even suns o'er autumn's bowers
           Heard my strong wish, and stayed.

They came and went, the short-lived four,
    Yet as their varying dance they wove,
        To my young heart each bore
           Its own sure claim of love

Far different now ;—the whirling year
　　Vainly my dizzy eyes pursue ;
　　　And its fair tints appear
　　　　All blent in one dusk hue.

Why dwell on rich autumnal lights,
　　Spring-time, or winter's social ring ?
　　　Long days are fire-side nights,
　　　　Brown autumn is fresh spring.

Then what this world to thee, my heart ?
　　Its gifts nor feed thee nor can bless ;
　　　Thou hast no owner's part
　　　　In all its fleetingness.

The flame, the storm, the quaking ground,
　　Earth's joy, earth's terror, nought is thine :
　　　Thou must but hear the sound
　　　　Of the still voice divine.

O princely lot! O blissful art !
　　E'en while by sense of change opprest,
　　　Thus to forecast in heart
　　　　Heaven's Age of fearless rest.

δ.

XLIV.

MELCHIZEDEK

Without father, without mother, without descent, having neither beginning of days nor end of life.

THRICE blest are they who feel their loneliness;
  To whom nor voice of friend nor pleasant scene
  Brings that on which the saddened heart can lean;
Yea, the rich earth, garbed in its daintiest dress
Of light and joy, doth but the more oppress,
  Claiming responsive smiles and rapture high:
  Till, sick at heart, beyond the vail they fly,
Seeking His presence, who alone can bless.
Such in strange days, the weapons of Heaven's grace;
When, passing o'er the highborn Hebrew line,
He forms the vessel of his vast design;
Fatherless, homeless, reft of age and place,
Severed from earth, and careless of its wreck,
Born through long woe His rare Melchizedek.

δ.

ANCIENT SCENES.

XLV.

SIREN ISLES

CEASE, Stranger, cease those piercing notes,
   The craft of Siren choirs;
Hush the seductive voice, that floats
   Upon the languid wires.

Music's ethereal fire was given,
   Not to dissolve our clay,
But draw Promethean beams from heaven,
   And purge the dross away.

Weak self! with thee the mischief lies,
   Those throbs a tale disclose;
Nor age nor trial have made wise
   The Man of many woes

                                  δ.

XLVI.

MESSENA

WHY, wedded to the Lord, still yearns my heart
   Upon these scenes of ancient heathen fame?
   Yet legend hoar, and voice of bard that came
Fixing my restless youth with its sweet heart,
And shades of power, and those who bore their part
   In the mad deeds that set the world in flame,
   So fret my memory here,—ah! is it blame—
That from my eyes the tear is fain to start?
Nay, from no fount impure these drops arise;
'Tis but the sympathy with Adam's race,
Which in each brother's history reads its own.
So, let the cliffs and seas of this fair place
Be named man's tomb and splendid record-stone,
High hope pride-stained, the course without the prize.

                                 δ.

XLVII.

TAUROMINIUM.

And Jacob went on his way, and the Angels of God met him.

SAY, hast thou tracked a traveller's round
    Nor visions met thee there,
Thou couldst but marvel to have found
    This blighted world so fair?

And feel an awe within thee rise,
    That sinful man should see
Glories far worthier Seraph's eyes
    Than to be shared by thee?

Store them in heart! thou shalt not faint
    'Mid coming pains and fears,
As the third heaven once nerved a Saint
    For fourteen trial years.

δ.

XLVIII.

CORCYRA.

I sat beneath an olive's branches grey
  And gazed upon the site of a lost town,
  By sage and poet chosen for renown ;
Where dwelt a Race that on the sea held sway,
And, restless as its waters, forced a way
  For civil strife a thousand states to drown.
That multitudinous stream we now note down,
As though one life, in birth and in decay.
Yet, is their being's history spent and run,
Whose spirits live in awful singleness,
Each in his self-formed sphere of light or gloom ?
Henceforth, while pondering the fierce deeds then done,
Such reverence on me shall its seal impress
As though I corpses saw, and walked the tomb.

δ.

BEREAVEMENT.

XLIX.

" Wherefore I abhor myself and repent in dust and ashes."
Job xlii 6.

AND dare I say, " Welcome to me
    The pang that proves thee near ?"
O words, too oft on bended knee
    Breath'd to th' Unerring Ear.
While the cold spirit silently
    Pines at the scourge severe.

Nay, try once more—thine eyelids close
    For prayer intense and meek :
When the warm light gleams thro' and shows
    Him near who helps the weak.
Unmurmuring then thy heart's repose
    In dust and ashes seek.

But when the self-abhoring thrill
  Is past, as pass it must,
When tasks of life thy spirit fill,
  Risen from thy tears and dust,
Then be the self-renouncing will
  The seal of thy calm trust.

γ.

I.

BURIAL OF THE DEAD.

I THOUGHT to meet no more, so dreary seem'd
Death's interposing veil, and thou so pure,
    Thy place in Paradise
    Beyond where I could soar ;

Friend of this worthless heart ! but happier thoughts
Spring like unbidden violets from the sod,
    Where patiently thou tak'st
    Thy sweet and sure repose.

The shadows fall more soothing : the soft air
Is full of cheering whispers like thine own ;
  While Memory, by thy grave,
  Lives o'er thy funeral day ;

The deep knell dying down, the mourners' pause
Waiting their Saviour's welcome at the gate.—
  Sure with the words of Heaven
  Thy spirit met us there,

And sought with us along th' accustomed way
The hallowed porch, and entering in, beheld
  The pageant of sad joy,
  So dear to Faith and Hope.

O ! hadst thou brought a strain from Paradise
To cheer us, happy soul, thou hadst not touched
  The sacred springs of grief
  More tenderly and true,

Than those deep-warbled anthems, high and low,
Low as the grave, high as th' Eternal Throne,
  Guiding through light and gloom
  Our mourning fancies wild,

Till gently, like soft golden clouds at eve
Around the western twilight, all subside
  Into a placid Faith,
  That even with beaming eye

Counts thy sad honours, coffin, bier, and pall;
So many relics of a frail love lost,
  So many tokens dear
  Of endless love begun.

Listen! it is no dream : th' Apostles' trump
Gives earnest of th' Archangel's ;—calmly now
  Our hearts yet beating high
  To that victorious lay.

Most like a warrior's to the martial dirge
Of a true comrade, in the grave we trust
  Our treasure for a while :
  And if a tear steal down,

If human anguish o'er the shaded brow
Pass shuddering, when the handful of pure earth
  Touches the coffin lid ;
  If at our brother's name,

G

Once and again the thought, "for ever gone,"
Come o'er us like a cloud; yet, gentle spright,
      Thou turnest not away,
      Thou knowest us calm at heart.

One look, and we have seen our last of thee,
Till we too sleep and our long sleep be o'er;
      O cleanse us, ere we view
      That countenance pure again,

THOU, who canst change the heart, and raise the dead;
As THOU art by to soothe our parting hour,
      Be ready when we meet,
      With Thy dear pardoning words.

γ.

SAINTS DEPARTED.

LI.

REMOVAL

DEAR sainted Friends, I call not you,
　　To share the joy serene
Which flows upon me from the view
　　Of crag and steep ravine.

Ye, on that loftier mountain old,
　　Safe lodged in Eden's cell,
Whence run the rivers four, behold
　　This earth, as ere it fell.

Or, when ye think of those who stay
    Still tried by the world's fight,
'Tis but in looking for the day
    Which shall the lost unite.

Ye rather, elder Spirits strong!
    Who from the first have trod
This nether scene, man's race among,
    The while ye live to God.

Ye hear, and ye can sympathize—
    Vain thought! those eyes of fire
Pierce thro' God's works, and duly prize;
    Ye smile when we admire.

Ah, Saviour Lord! with thee my heart
    Angel nor Saint shall share;
To thee 'tis known, for man Thou art,
    To soothe each tumult there

                                        δ

LII.

REST.

THEY are at rest:
We may not stir the heaven of their repose
By rude invoking voice, or prayer addrest
    In waywardness to those,
Who in the mountain grots of Eden lie,
And hear the fourfold river as it murmurs by.

    They hear it sweep
In distance down the dark and savage vale;
But they at rocky bed, or current deep,
    Shall never more grow pale;
They hear, and meekly muse, as fain to know
How long untired, unspent, that giant stream shall flow.

    And soothing sounds
Blend with the neighbouring waters as they glide;
Posted along the haunted garden's bounds,
    Angelic forms abide,
Echoing, as words of watch, o'er lawn and grove
The verses of that hymn which Seraphs chant above.

                  δ.

LIII.

KNOWLEDGE.

WEEP not for me ;—
Be blithe as wont, nor tinge with gloom
The stream of love that circles home,
Light hearts and free !
Joy in the gifts Heaven's bounty lends ;
Nor miss my face, dear friends !

I still am near ;—
Watching the smiles I prized on earth,
Your converse mild, your blameless mirth ;
Now too I hear,
Of whisper'd sounds the tale complete,
Low prayers, and musings sweet.

A sea before
The Throne is spread ; its pure, still glass
Pictures all earth-scenes as they pass.
We, on its shore,
Share in the bosom of our rest,
God's knowledge, and are blest !

δ.

LIV.

PRAYER.

WHILE Moses on the Mountain lay,
Night after night, and day by day,
 Till forty suns were gone,
Unconscious, in the Presence bright,
Of lustrous day and starry night,
As though his soul had flitted quite
 From earth, and Eden won;

The pageant of a kingdom vast,
And things unutterable, past
 Before the Prophet's eye;
Dread shadows of the Eternal Throne,
The fount of Life, and Altar-stone,
Pavement, and them that tread thereon,
 And those who worship nigh.

But lest he should his own forget,
Who in the vale were struggling yet,
 A sadder vision came,
Announcing all that guilty deed
Of idol rite, that in her need
He for the Church might intercede,
 And stay Heaven's rising flame.

      δ.

HIDDEN SAINTS.

LV.

HID are the Saints of God;
Uncertified by high angelic sign;
Nor raiment soft, nor empire's golden rod
    Marks them divine.
Theirs but the unbought air, earth's parent sod,
    And the sun's smile benign ;—
Christ rears His throne within the secret heart,
    From the haughty world apart.

They gleam amid the night,
Chill sluggish mists stifling the heavenly ray ;
Fame chants the while,—old history trims his light,
     Aping the day ;
In vain ! staid look, loud voice, and reason's might
    Forcing its learned way,
Blind characters ! these aid us not to trace
    Christ and His princely race.

Yet not all-hid from those
Who watch to see ;—'neath their dull guise of earth,
Bright bursting gleams unwittingly disclose
     Their heaven-wrought birth.
Meekness, love, patience, faith's serene repose ;
    And the soul's tutored mirth,
Bidding the slow heart dance, to prove her power
    O'er self in its proud hour.

These are the chosen few,
The remnant fruit of largely-scattered grace.
God sows in waste, to reap whom he foreknew
    Of man's cold race :
Counting on wills perverse, in His clear view
    Of boundless time and space,
He waits, by scant return for treasures given,
    To fill the thrones of heaven.

Lord ! who can trace but Thou
The strife obscure, 'twixt sin's soul-thralling spell,
And thy sharp Spirit, now quenched, reviving now ?
    Or who can tell,
Why pardon's seal stands sure on David's brow,
    Why Saul and Demas fell ?
Oh ! lest our frail hearts in the annealing break,
    Help, for Thy mercy's sake !

                          δ.

LVI.

ISAAC.

MANY the guileless years the Patriarch spent,
   Blessed in the wife a father's foresight chose ;
   Many the prayers and gracious deeds, which rose
Daily thank-offerings from his pilgrim tent.
Yet these, though written in the heavens, are rent
   From out truth's lower roll, which sternly shews
   But one sad trespass at his history's close,
Father's, son's, mother's, and its punishment.
Not in their brightness, but their earthly stains
Are the true seed vouchsafed to earthly eyes.
Sin can read sin, but dimly scans high grace,
   So we move heavenward with averted face,
Scared into faith by warning of sin's pains ;
And Saints are lowered, that the world may rise.

δ.

LVII.

THE CALL OF DAVID.

" And the Lord said, Arise, anoint him, for this is he."

LATEST born of Jesse's race,
Wonder lights thy bashful face,
While the prophet's gifted oil
Seals thee for a path of toil.
We, thy Angels, circling round thee,
Ne'er shall find thee as we found thee,
When thy faith first brought us near
In thy lion-fight severe.

Go ! and mid thy flocks awhile
At thy doom of greatness smile ;
Bold to bear God's heaviest load,
Dimly guessing of the road,—
Rocky road, and scarce ascended,
Though thy foot be angel-tended !

Double praise thou shalt attain,
In royal court and battle plain;
Then comes heart-ache, care, distress,
Blighted hope, and loneliness;
Wounds from friend and gifts from foe,
Dizzied faith, and guilt, and woe,
Loftiest aims by earth defiled,
Gleams of wisdom sin-beguiled,
Sated power's tyrannic mood,
Counsels shared with men of blood,
Sad success, parental tears,
And a dreary gift of years.

Strange, that guileless face and form
To lavish on the scarring storm!
Yet we take thee in thy blindness,
And we harass thee in kindness;
Little chary of thy fame,—
Dust unborn may bless or blame,—
But we mould thee for the root
Of man's promised healing fruit,
And we mould thee hence to rise
As our brother to the skies.

δ.

LVIII.

"They glorified God in me."

I saw thee once, and nought discerned
　　For stranger to admire ;
A serious aspect, but it burned
　　With no unearthly fire.

Again I saw, and I confessed
　　Thy speech was rare and high ;
And yet it vexed my burdened breast,
　　And scared, I knew not why.

I saw once more, and awe-struck gazed
　　On face, and form, and air ;
God's living glory round thee blazed—
　　A Saint—a Saint was there !

　　　　　　　　　δ.

LIX.

I fear, lest, when I come, I shall not find you such as I would,
and that I shall be found unto you such as ye would not.

I DREAMED that, with a passionate complaint,
  I wished me born amid God's deeds of might ;
  And envied those who saw the presence bright
Of gifted Prophet and strong-hearted saint,
Whom my heart loves, and fancy strives to paint.
  I turned, when straight a stranger met my sight,
  Came as my guest, and did awhile unite
His lot with mine, and lived without restraint.
Courteous he was, and grave,—so meek in mien,
It seemed untrue, or told a purpose weak ;
Yet in the mood, he could with aptness speak,
Or with stern force, or show of feelings keen,
Marking deep craft, methought, or hidden pride :
Then came a voice—" St. Paul is at thy side !"

δ.

LIGHTING OF LAMPS.

LX.

" And Aaron shall burn thereon sweet incense every morning when he dresseth the lamps he shall burn incense upon it. And when Aaron lighteth the lamps at even, he shall burn incense upon it; a perpetual incense before the Lord, throughout your generations."

Now the stars are lit in heaven,
 We must light our lamps on earth:
Every star a signal given
 From the God of our new birth:
Every lamp an answer faint,
Like the prayer of mortal Saint.

Mark the hour and turn this way,
 Sons of Israel, far and near!
Wearied with the world's dim day,
 Turn to Him whose eyes are here,
Open, watching day and night,
Beaming unapproached light!

With sweet oil-drops in His hour
   Feed the branch of many lights,
Token of protecting power,
   Pledg'd to faithful Israelites,
Emblem of th' anointed Home,
When the glory deigns to come.

Watchers of the sacred flame,
   Sons of Aaron! serve in fear,—
Deadly is th' avenger's aim,
   Should th' unhallowed enter here;
Keen His fires, should recreants dare
Breathe the pure and fragrant air.

There is One will bless your toil—
   He who comes in Heaven's attire,
Morn by morn, with holy oil;
   Eve by eve, with holy fire!
Pray!—your prayer will be allowed,
Mingling with His incense cloud!

γ.

LXI.

"Then spake Jesus again unto them, saying, I am the Light of the world: he that followeth Me shall not walk in darkness, but shall have the light of life."

FULL many an eve, and many a morn,
　　The holy Lamps have blazed and died;
The floor by knees of sinners worn,
The mystic Altar's golden horn,
Age after age have witness borne
To faith that on a lingering Saviour cried.

"At evening time there shall be light"—
　　'Twas said of old—'tis wrought to-day:
Now, with the stoled Priest in sight,
The perfumed embers quivering bright,
Ere yet the ceiling's spangled height
The glory catch of the new-kindled ray!

A voice not loud, but thrilling clear,
  On hearts prepared, falls benign :—
" I am the world's true Light : who hear
And follow Me, no darkness fear,
Nor waning eve, nor changing year,
The light of Life is theirs : pure Light of Life divine!"

γ.

LXII.

" And there were many lights in the upper chamber where they
were gathered together."

HE spake : He died and rose again—
  And now his Spirit lights
The hallowed fires o'er land and main,
  And every heart invites.

They glow : but not in gems and gold
  With cedar arched o'er ;
But in far nooks obscure and cold,
  On many a cabin floor :

When the true soldiers steal an hour
  To break the bread of Life,
And drink the draught of love and power,
  And plan the holy strife.

Ye humble Tapers, fearless burn—
  Ere in the morn ye fade,
Ye shall behold a soul return,
  Even from the last dim shade.

That all may know what love untold
  Attends the chosen race,
Whom apostolic arms enfold,
  Who cling to that embrace:

And wheresoe'er a cottage light
  Is trimmed for evening prayer,
Faith may recall that wondrous night—
  Who raised the dead, is there.

7.

LXIII.

H<small>AIL</small>! gladdening L<small>IGHT</small>, of His pure glory poured
Who is th' immortal F<small>ATHER</small>, heavenly, blest,
Holiest of Holies—J<small>ESUS</small> C<small>HRIST</small> our L<small>ORD</small>!
Now we are come to the sun's hour of rest,
The lights of evening round us shine,
We hymn the F<small>ATHER</small>, S<small>ON</small>, and H<small>OLY</small> S<small>PIRIT</small> divine!
Worthiest art Thou at all times to be sung
With undefiled tongue,
S<small>ON</small> of our G<small>OD</small>, Giver of Life, alone!
Therefore in all the world, thy glories, L<small>ORD</small>, they
own.*

γ.

---

* *Hymn of the 1st or 2nd Century: preserved by St. Basil.—*
[*Vid. Routh Relliqu. Sacr.* iii. *p.* 299.]

φῶς ἱλαρὸν ἁγίας δόξης ἀθανάτου Πατρὸς,
Οὐρανίου, ἁγίου, μάκαρος,
Ἰησοῦ Χριστὲ,
ἐλθόντες ἐπὶ τοῦ ἡλίου δύσιν,
ἰδόντες φῶς ἑσπερινόν,
ὑμνοῦμεν Πατέρα, καὶ Υἱὸν, καὶ Ἅγιον Πνεῦμα Θεοῦ,
ἄξιος εἶ ἐν πᾶσι καιροῖς ὑμνεῖσθαι φωναῖς ὁσίαις
Υἱὲ Θεοῦ, ζωὴν ὁ διδούς·
διὸ ὁ κοσμός σε δοξάζει.

LXIV.

THE CHURCHMAN TO HIS LAMP.

Come, twinkle in my lonely room,
Companion true in hours of gloom ;
Come, light me on a little space,
The heavenly vision to retrace,
By Saints and Angels loved so well,—
My Mother's glories ere she fell.

There was a time, my friendly Lamp,
When, far and wide, in Jesus' camp,
Oft as the foe dark inroads made,
They watched and fasted, wept and pray'd,
But now, they feast and slumber on,
And say, " Why pine o'er evil done ?"

Then hours of Prayer, in welcome round,
Far-severed hearts together bound ;
Seven times a day, *on bended knee*,
They to their Saviour cried ; and we—

One hour we find in seven long days,
Before our God to *sit* and *gaze!*

Then, lowly Lamp, a ray like thine
Waked half the world to hymns divine,
Now it is much if here and there
One dreamer, by the genial glare,
Trace the dim Past, and slowly climb
The steep of Faith's triumphant prime.

Yet by His grace, whose breathing gives
Life to the faintest spark that lives,
I trim thee, precious Lamp, once more,
Our fathers' armoury to explore,
And sort and number wistfully
A few bright weapons, bath'd on high.

And may thy guidance ever tend
Where gentle thoughts with courage blend :
Thy pure and steady gleaming rest
On pages with the Cross imprest ;
Till, touch'd with lightning of calm zeal,
Our fathers' very heart we feel.

SOBRIETY.

LXV.

Him that escapeth from the sword of Jehu, shall Elisha slay.

CHRIST bade his followers take the sword,
 And yet He chid the deed,
When Peter seized upon His word,
 And made a foe to bleed.

The gospel Creed, a sword of strife,
 Meek hands alone may rear;
And ever Zeal begins its life
 In silent thought and fear.

Ye, who would weed the Vineyard's soil,
 Treasure the lesson given;
Lest in the judgment-books ye toil
 For Satan, not for heaven.

δ.

LXVI.

"Come with me, and see my zeal for the LORD."

Thou to wax fierce
   In the cause of the LORD,
To threat and to pierce
   With the heavenly sword!
Anger and Zeal,
   And the Joy of the brave,
Whe bade *thee* to feel,
    Sin's slave.

The Altar's pure flame
   Consumes as it soars;
Faith meetly may blame,
   For it serves and adores.
Thou warnest and smitest!
   Yet CHRIST must atone
For a soul that thou slightest—
   Thine own.

δ.

LXVII.

THY words are good and freely given,
　As though thou felt them true ;
Friend, think thee well, to hell or heaven
　A serious heart is due.

It pains thee sore, man's will should swerve
　In his true path divine ;
And yet thou venturest not to serve
　Thy neighbour's weal nor thine.

Beware ! such words may once be said,
　Where shame and fear unite ;
But, spoken twice, they mark instead
　A sin against the light.

δ.

LXVIII.

DEEDS NOT WORDS.

PRUNE thou thy words, the thoughts control
   That o'er thee swell and throng ;
They will condense within thy soul,
   And change to purpose strong.

But he, who lets his feelings run
   In soft luxurious flow,
Shrinks when hard service must be done,
   And faints at every woe.

Faith's meanest deed more favour bears,
   Where hearts and wills are weighed,
Than brightest transports, choicest prayers,
   Which bloom their hour and fade.

δ.

LXIX.

I have need to be baptized of Thee, and comest Thou to me?

How didst thou start, Thou Holy Baptist, bid
   To pour repentance on the Sinless Brow!
Then all thy meekness, from thy hearers hid,
   Beneath the Ascetic's port, and Preacher's fire,
Flowed forth, and with a pang thou didst desire
     He might be chief, not thou.

And so on us, at whiles, it falls to claim
   Powers that we fear, or dare some forward part;
Nor must we shrink as cravens from the blame
   Of pride, in common eyes, or purpose deep;
But with pure thoughts look up to God, and keep
     Our secret in our heart.

                             δ.

AMBITION.

LXX.

SLEEP.

UNWEARIED God, before whose face
   The night is clear as day,
Whilst we, poor worms, o'er life's brief race
   Now creep, and now delay;
We with death's foretaste alternate
Our labour's dint and sorrow's weight,
Save, in that fever-troubled state
   When pain and care hold sway.

Dread Lord ! Thy glory, watchfulness,
　Is but disease in man ;
Oh ! hence upon our hearts impress
　Our place in the world's plan !
Pride grasps the powers by Heaven displayed ;
But ne'er the rebel effort made
But fell beneath the sudden shade
　Of nature's withering ban.

　　　　　　　　　　　　　　δ.

LXXI.

THE ELEMENTS.

πολλὰ τὰ δεῖνα, χοὐδὲν
ἀνθρώπου δεινότερον πέλει.

MAN is permitted much
　To scan and learn
　In Nature's frame ;
Till he well-nigh can tame
Brute mischiefs, and can touch
Invisible things, and turn
All warring ills to purposes of good.

Thus as a God below,
    He can control,
And harmonize what seems amiss to flow
    As severed from the whole
    And dimly understood.

    But o'er the elements
      One Hand alone
      One Hand has sway.
    What influence day by day
    In straiter belt prevents
 ' The impious Ocean, thrown
Alternate o'er the ever-sounding shore?
    Or who has eye to trace
      How the Plague came ?
Forerun the doublings of the Tempest's race ?
    Or the Air's weight and flame
    On a set scale explore ?

 '   Thus God has willed
That man, when fully skilled

Still gropes in twilight dim ,
Encompassed all his hours
   By fearfullest powers
   Inflexible to him ;
That so he may discern
   His feebleness,
   And e'en for earth's success
To Him in wisdom turn,
Who holds for us the Keys of either home,
   Earth and the world to come.

δ.

ACTIVITY.

LXXII.

" Freely ye have received : freely give."

" Give any boon for peace !
Why should our fair-eyed Mother e'er engage
In the world's course and on a troubled stage,
From which her very call is a release ?
　　No ! in thy garden stand,
　　And tend with pious hand
　　The flowers thou findest there,
　　Which are thy proper care,
O man of God ! in meekness and in love,
And waiting for the blissful realms above."

Alas ! for thou must learn,
Thou guileless one ! rough is the holy hand ;
Runs not the Word of Truth through every land,
A sword to sever, and a fire to burn ?
    If blessed Paul had stayed
    In cot or learned shade,
    With the priest's white attire,
    And the saints' tuneful choir,
Men had not gnashed their teeth, nor risen to slay,
But thou hadst been a heathen in thy day.
                                    δ.

LXXIII.

Time was, I shrank from what was right,
    From fear of what was wrong ;
I would not brave the sacred fight,
    Because the foe was strong.

But now I cast that finer sense
    And sorer shame aside ;
Such dread of sin was indolence,
    Such aim at heaven was pride.

So, when my Saviour calls, I rise
    And calmly do my best ;
Leaving to Him, with silent eyes
    Of hope and fear, the rest.

I step, I mount where He has led ;
    Men count my haltings o'er ;—
I know them ; yet, though self I dread,
    I love His precept more.

                                  ẟ.

LXXIV.

ΠΑΥΛΟΥ ΜΙΜΗΤΗΣ.

O LORD ! when sin's close marshalled line
    Urges thy witness on his way,
How should he raise Thy glorious Sign,
    And how Thy will display ?

Thy holy Paul, with soul of flame,
    Rose on Mars'-hill, a soldier lone ;
Shall I thus speak the Atoning Name,
    Though with a heart of stone ?

" Not so," He said .—" hush thee, and seek,
　With thoughts in prayer and watchful eyes,
My seasons sent for thee to speak,
　And use them as they rise."

　　　　　　　　　　　　　　　　ε.

LXXV.

THE SAINT AND THE HERO

O AGED Saint! far off I heard
　The praises of thy name ;
Thy deed of power, thy skilful word,
　Thy zeal's triumphant flame.

I came and saw ; and, having seen,
　Weak heart, I drew offence
From thy prompt smile, thy simple mien,
　Thy lowly diligence.

The Saint's is not the Hero's praise ;—
　This have I found, and learn
Nor to profane Heaven's humblest ways,
　Nor its least boon to spurn.

　　　　　　　　　　　　　　　　ε.

EASE.

LXXVI.

THE WATCH BY NIGHT.

"And Uriah said unto David, The ark, and Israel, and Judah, abide in tents; and my lord Joab, and the servants of my lord, are encamped in the open fields; shall I then go into mine house, to eat and to drink?....As thou livest, and as thy soul liveth, I will not do this thing."

THE Ark of God is in the field,
Like clouds around the alien armies sweep;
Each by his spear, beneath his shield,
In cold and dew the anointed warriors sleep.

And can it be thou liest awake,
Sworn watchman, tossing on thy couch of down?
And doth thy recreant heart not ache
To hear the sentries round the leaguered town?

K

Oh dream no more of quiet life ;

Care finds the careless out : more wise to vow

Thine heart entire to Faith's pure strife ;

So peace will come, thou knowest not when or how.

7.

LXXVII.

JONAH.

"But Jonah rose up to flee unto Tarshish, from the presence of
the Lord."

DEEP in his meditative bower,

The tranquil seer reclined ;

Numbering the creepers of an hour,

The gourds which o'er him twined.

To note each plant, to rear each fruit

Which soothes the languid sense,

He deemed a safe refined pursuit,—

His LORD, an indolence.

The sudden voice was heard at length,

" Lift thou the prophet's rod !"

But sloth had sapped the prophet's strength,

He feared, and fled from GOD.

Next, by a fearful judgment tamed,
   He threats the offending race ;
God spares ;—he murmurs, pride-inflamed,
   His threat made void by grace.

What ?—pride and sloth ! man's worst of foes !
   And can such guests invade
Our choicest bliss, the green repose
   Of the sweet garden-shade ?

δ.

LXXVIII.

JEREMIAH

"Oh, that I had in the wilderness a lodging-place of wayfaring
men, that I might leave my people and go from them."

"Woe's me !" the peaceful prophet cried,
   "Spare me this troubled life ;
To stem man's wrath, to school his pride,
   To head the sacred strife !

" O place me in some silent vale,
    Where groves and flowers abound ;
Nor eyes that grudge, nor tongues that rail,
    Vex the truth-haunted ground !"

If his meek spirit erred, opprest
    That God denied repose,
What sin is ours, to whom Heaven's rest
    Is pledged to heal earth's woes ?

δ.

LXXIX.

New Self.

WHY sittest thou on that sea-girt rock
With downward look and sadly dreaming eye ?
    Playest thou beneath with Proteus' flock,
Or with the far-bound sea-bird wouldest thou fly ?

Old Self.

I sit upon this sea-girt rock
With downward look and dreaming eye,
    But neither do I sport with Proteus' flock,
Nor with the far-bound sea-bird would I fly.

I list the splash so clear and chill
Of yon old fisher's solitary oar :
 I watch the waves that rippling still
Chase one another o'er the marble shore.

New Self.

Yet from the splash of yonder oar
No dreamy sound of sadness comes to me :
 And yon fresh waves that beat the shore,
How merrily they splash, how merrily !

Old Self.

I mourn for the delicious days,
When those calm sounds fell on my childish ear,
 A stranger yet to the wild ways
Of triumph and remorse, of hope and fear.

New Self.

Mournest thou, poor soul, and wouldest thou yet
Call back the things which shall not, cannot be ;
 Heaven must be won, not dreamed ; thy task is set,
Peace was not made for earth, nor rest for thee.*

β.

---

* Hæc memini, et victum frustra contendere Thyrsin,
Ex illo Corydon, Corydon est tempore nobis.

LXXX.

ST. PAUL AT MELITA.

" And when Paul had gathered a bundle of sticks, and laid them
on the fire, there came a viper out of the heat."

SECURE in his prophetic strength,
    The water peril o'er,
The many-gifted man at length
    Stepped on the promised shore.

He trod the shore ; but not to rest,
    Nor wait till Angels came ;
Lo ! humblest pains the Saint attest,
    The firebrands and the flame.

But, when he felt the viper's smart,
    Then instant aid was given ;
Christian ! hence learn to do thy part,
    And leave the rest to heaven.

δ.

SEVERITY.

LXXXI.

" Am I my brother's keeper ?"

THE time has been, it seemed a precept plain
    Of the true faith, Christ's tokens to display;
And in life's commerce still the thought retain,
    That men have souls, and wait a judgment-day;
Kings used their gifts as ministers of heaven,
Nor stripped their zeal for God, of means which God
      had given.

'Tis altered now ;—for Adam's eldest born
    Has trained our practice in a selfish rule ,
Each stands alone, Christ's bonds asunder torn,
    Each has his private thought, selects his school,
Conceals his creed, and lives in closest tie
Of fellowship with those who count it blasphemy.

Brothers! spare reasoning,—men have settled long
   That ye are out of date, and they are wise ;
Use their own weapons; let your words be strong,
   Your cry be loud, till each scared boaster flies ;
Thus the Apostles tamed the pagan breast,
They argued not, but preached; and conscience did
   the rest.

                         δ.

LXXXII.

ZEAL BEFORE LOVE.

AND wouldst thou reach, rash scholar mine,
   Love's high unruffled state ?
Awake ! thy easy dreams resign :
   First learn thee how to hate.

Hatred of sin, and Zeal, and Fear,
   Lead up the Holy Hill ;
Track them, till Charity appear
   A self-denial still.

Feeble and false the brightest flame
 By thoughts severe unfed ;
Book-lore ne'er served, when trial came,
 Nor gifts, where faith was dead

      δ.

LXXXIII.

THE WRATH TO COME

WHEN first God stirred me, and the Church's word
 Came as a theme of reverent search and fear,
 It little cost to own the lustre clear
O'er rule she taught, and rite, and doctrine poured ;
For conscience craved, and reason did accord.
 Yet one there was that wore a mien austere,
 And I did doubt, and, troubled, asked to hear
Whose mouth had force to edge so sharp a sword.
My Mother oped her trust, the Holy Book,
And healed my pang. She pointed, and I found
Christ on Himself, considerate Master, took
The utterance of that doctrine's fearful sound.
The fount of Love His servants sends to tell
Love's deeds ; Himself reveals the sinner's hell.

      δ.

CHRISTIAN CHIVALRY.

LXXXIV.

1.

" Silence, unworthy! how should tones like thine
Blend with the warnings of the good and true?
God hath no need of waverers round His shrine :
What hath th'unclean with Heaven's high cause to do?"
Thus in the deep of many a shrinking heart
The murmurings swell and heave of sad remorse ;
And dull the soul, that else would keenly dart
Fearless along her heaven-illumined course.
But, wayward doubter, lift one glance on high ;
What banner streams along thy destin'd way ?

The pardoning Cross,—His Cross who deign'd to die
To cleanse th' impure for His own bright array.
Wash thee in His dear blood, and trembling wear
His holy Sign, and take thy station there.

2.

Wash thee, and watch thine armour; as of old
The champions vow'd of Truth and Purity,
Ere the bright mantle might their limbs enfold,
Or spear of theirs in knightly combat vie,
Three summer nights outwatch'd the stars on high,
And found the time too short for busy dreams,
Pageants of airy prowess dawning nigh,
And fame far hovering with immortal beams.
And more than prowess theirs, and more than fame;
No dream, but an abiding consciousness
Of an approving God, a righteous aim,
An arm outstretch'd to guide them and to bless:
Firm as steel bows for Angel's warfare bent
They went abroad, not knowing where they went.

3.

For why? the sacred Pentecostal eve
Had bath'd them with its own inspiring dew,
And gleams more bright than summer sunsets leave
Lingering well-nigh to meet the morn's fresh hue,
Dwelt on each heart; as erst in memory true,
The Spirit's chosen heralds o'er all lands
Bore the bright tongues of fire. Thus, firm and few,
Now, in our fallen time, might faithful bands
Move on th' eternal way, the goal in sight,
Nor to the left hand swerve for gale or shower,
Nor pleasure win them, wavering to the right,
Alone with Heaven they were that awful hour,
When their oath seal'd them to the war of Faith:
Alone they will be in the hour of death.

7.

LONELINESS.

LXXXV.

THE COURSE OF TRUTH.

" Him God raised up the third day, and shewed Him openly,
not to all the people, but unto witnesses chosen before of God."

WHEN royal Truth, released from mortal throes,
Burst His brief slumber, and triumphant rose, ,
    Ill had the Holiest sued
    A patron multitude,
Or courted Tetrarch's eye, or claimed to rule
By the world's winning grace, or proofs from learned
    school.

But, robing Him in viewless air, He told
His secret to a few of meanest mould;
  They in their turn imparted
  The gift to men pure-hearted.
While the brute many heard His mysteries high,
As some strange fearful tongue, and crouched the
  knew not why.

Still is the might of Truth, as it has been:
Lodged in the few, obeyed, and yet unseen.
  Reared on lone heights, and rare,
  His saints their watch-flame bear,
And the mad world sees the wide-circling blaze,
Vain-searching whence it streams, and how to quenc
  its rays.
          ﬡ.

LXXXVI.

Time was, though truth eterne I felt my creed,
That when men smiled and said, "thy words ai
  strong,
But others think not thus; and dar'st thou plead
That thou art right, and all beside thee wrong?"
I shrunk abashed, nor dared the theme prolong.

Now, in that creed's most high and holy strain
Led to revere the Church's solemn tone,
The calm, clear accents of the chosen One,
Christ's mystic Bride, oi dained with him to reign,
I hear with pitying sigh such taunts profane ;
Taught that my faith, in hers, is based secure
On the unshaken Rock, that shall for aye endure.

a.

LXXXVII.

THE WATCHMAN

" Quit you like men, be strong."

Faint not, and fret not, for threatened woe,
    Watchman on Truth's grey height !
Few though the faithful, and fierce though the foe,
    Weakness is aye Heaven's might.

Infidel Ammon and niggard Tyre,
    Ill-attuned pair, unite ;
Some work for love, and some work for hire,
    But weakness shall be Heaven's might !

Eli's feebleness, Saul's black wrath,
    May aid Ahitophel's spite ,
And prayers from Gerizim, and curses from Gath...
    Our weakness shall be Heaven's might.

Quail not, and quake not, thou Warder bold,
    Be there no friend in sight ;
Turn thee to question the days of old,
    When weakness was aye Heaven's might.

Moses was one, yet he stayed the sin
    Of the host, in the Presence bright ;
And Elias scorned the Carmel-din,
    When Baal would scan Heaven's might.

Time's years are many, Eternity one,
    And one is the Infinite ;
The chosen are few, few the deeds well done,
    For scantness is still Heaven's might.

$\delta.$

LXXXVIII.

VEXATIONS.

Each trial has its weight; which whoso bears,
    Knows his own woe, and need of succouring
        grace :
    The martyr's hope half wipes away the trace
Of flowing blood; the while life's humblest cares
Smart more, because they hold in Holy Writ no place.

This be my comfort, in these days of grief
    Which is not Christ's, nor forms heroic tale.
    Apart from Him, if not a sparrow fail,
May not He pitying view, and send relief
When foes or friends perplex, and peevish thoughts
        prevail.

Then keep good heart; nor take the selfwise course
    Of Thomas, who must see ere he would trust.
    Faith will fill up God's word, not poorly just
To the bare letter, heedless of its force,
But walking by its light amid earth's sun and dust.

                       δ.

LXXXIX.

THE WINTER THRUSH.

Sweet bird! up earliest in the morn,
  Up earliest in the year,
Far in the quiet mist are borne,
  Thy matins soft and clear.

As linnet soft, and clear as lark,
  Well hast thou ta'en thy part,
Where many an ear thy notes may reach,
  And here and there a heart.

The first snow wreaths are scarcely gone
  (They staid but half a day)
The berries bright hang ling'ring on;
  Yet thou hast learned thy lay.

One gleam, one gale of western air
  Has hardly brush'd thy wing;
Yet thou hast given thy welcome fair,
  Good-morrow to the spring!

Perhaps within thy carol's sound
  Some wakeful mourner lies,
Dim roaming, days and years around,
  That ne'er again may rise.

He thanks thee with a tearful eye,
  For thou hast wing'd his spright
Back to some hour when hopes were nigh
  And dearest friends in sight:

That simple, fearless note of thine
  Has pierced the cloud of care,
And lit awhile the gleam divine
  That blessed his infant prayer;

Ere he had known, his faith to blight,
  The scorner's withering smile;
While hearts, he deem'd, beat true and right,
  Here in our Christian Isle.

That sunny, morning glimpse is gone,
  That morning note is still;
The dun dark day comes lowering on,
  The spoilers roam at will;

Yet calmly rise, and boldly strive;
 The sweet bird's early song,
Ere evening fall shall oft revive,
 And cheer thee all day long.

Are we not sworn to serve our King?
 He sworn with us to be?
The birds that chant before the spring,
 Are truer far than we.

γ.

COMMUNE DOCTORUM.

XC.

HAIL, glorious Lights, kindled at God's own urn,
Salt of the nations—whence the soul imbue
Savours of Godbead, virtues pure and true,
So that all die not—whence serenely burn
In their bright Orbs sure Truth and Virtue bold,
Putting on virgin honours undefiled :
Bounteous by you the World's Deliverer mild   .
Of treasured wisdom deals His stores untold.
Hail! channels where the living waters flow,
Whence the Redeemer's field shews fair, and glow
The golden harvests : ye from realms above
Bring meat for manly hearts, and milk for babes in
      love.

These bear, great God, thy sword and shield ;
These rear th' eternal Palace Hall ;
Skill'd with one hand Thine arms to wield,
   With one to build Thy Wall.
Ye in your bright celestial panoply
   O'ercame dark Heresy :
And when her brood from Stygian night
   Renew the fight,
We too may grasp your arrows bright,
E'en till this hour we combat in your mail,
And with no doubtful end,—we combat and prevail.
Hail ! Heavenly truth, guiding the pen
   Of wise and holy men ;
To thee, though thou be voiceless, doth belong
   A spirit's tongue,
Which in the heart's deep home, uttereth a song.*

                                   ζ.

* *(From the Paris Breviary.)*

Vos succensa Deo splendida Lumina :
Vos Sal, nos homines quo sapimus Deum :
Ævum puri animo moribus integri
   Quo condimur in alterum :

XCI.

THE GREEK FATHERS.

Let others sing thy heathen praise,
Fallen Greece! the thought of holier days
In my sad heart abides;

Per vos Relligio, tutaque Veritas
Per vos virgineis fulget honoribus :
Per vos Christus amat pandere divites
    Thesauros Sapientiæ.
Vestris unda fluit pura canalibus :
Christi floret ager; munda nitet seges;
Lac aptum pueris et solidum viris
Cauti sufficitis cibum.
Hi sunt, Summe Deus, qui tibi militant :
Hi sunt, qui stabiles ædificant domos :
Unâ docta cohors arma tenet manu,
    Muros construit alterâ.
Vicistis Stygias vos quibus Hæreses,
Hæc nos accipimus tela superstites :
His pugnamus adhuc, nec dubio exitu;
    His armis quoque vincimus.
Sit suprema tibi gloria, Veritas,
Quæ per scripta Patrum, quando foris sonas,
Nullo, vocis egens, corda doces sono;
    Et te mentibus inseris.

For sons of thine in Truth's first hour
Were tongues and weapons of his power,
Born of the Spirit's fiery shower,
   Our fathers and our guides.

All thine is Clement's varied page;
And Dionysius, ruler sage,
   In days of doubt and pain;
And Origen with eagle eye;
And saintly Basil's purpose high
To smite imperial heresy,
   And cleanse the Altar's stain.

From thee the glorious Preacher came
With soul of zeal and lips of flame,
   A court's stern martyr-guest;
And thine, O inexhaustive race!
Was Nazianzen's heaven-taught grace,
And royal-hearted Athanase,
   With Paul's own mantle blest.

                                           δ.

XCII.

CLEMENT.

METHOUGHT I saw a face divinely fair,
   With nought of earthly passion ; the mild beam
   Of whose bright eye did in mute converse seem
With other countenances, and they were
   Gazing on her made beautiful.   Their theme
Was One that had gone up the heavenly stair,
And left a fragrance on this lower air,
   The contemplation of His Love Supreme.
And that high form held forth to me a hand ;
It was celestial Wisdom, whose calm brow
Did of those early Sciences inquire,
If they had of His glory aught retained ;—
Yes ! I would be admitted to your choir,
That I may nothing love on earth below.

                              ζ.

XCIII.

ORIGEN.

INTO God's word as in a palace fair
Thou leadest on and on, while still beyond
Each chamber, touch'd by holy wisdom's wand,
Another opes, more beautiful and rare,
And thou in each art kneeling down in prayer,
From link to link of that mysterious bond
Seeking for Christ; but oh, I fear thy fond
And beautiful torch that with so bright a glare
Lighteth up all things, lest the heaven-lit brand
Of thy serene Philosophy divine
Should take the colourings of earthly thought,
And I, by their sweet images o'er-wrought,
Led by weak Fancy should let go Truth's hand
And miss the way into the inner shrine.

ς.

XCIV

ATHANASIUS.

WHEN shall our northern Church her champion see,
    Raised by divine decree,
To shield the Ancient Truth at his own harm? . . .
    Like him who stayed the arm
Of tyrannous power, and learning's sophist-tone,
    Keen-visioned Seer, alone.

The many crouched before an idol-priest,
    Lord of the world's rank feast.
In the dark night, mid the saints' trial sore,
    He stood, then bowed before
The Holy Mysteries,—he their meetest sign,
    Weak vessel, yet divine.*

Cyprian is ours, since the high-souled primate laid
    Under the traitorous blade

---

* Vid the account of Syrianus breaking Into his Church,
Theodoret Hist. II. 13.

His silvered head.   And Chrysostom we claim
  In that clear eloquent flame
And deep-taught zeal in the same woe, which shone
  Bright round a Martyr's throne.

And Ambrose reared his crosier as of old
  Less honoured, but as bold,
When in dark times our champion crossed a king :—
  But good in every thing
Comes as ill's cure.   Dim Future ! shall we NEED
  A prophet for Truth's Creed ?

          $\delta.$

XCV.

GREGORIUS THEOLOGUS.

PEACE-LOVING man, of humble heart and true !
  What dost thou here ?
Fierce is the city's crowd ; the lordly few
  Are dull of ear !
Sore pain it was to thee, till thou didst quit
Thy patriarch-throne at length, as though for power
 unfit.

So works the All-wise ! our services dividing
    Not as we ask ;
For the world's profit, by our gifts deciding
    Our duty-task.
See in king's courts loth Jeremiah plead ;
And slow-tongued Moses rule by eloquence of deed !

Yes ! thou, bright Angel of the East, didst rear
    The Cross divine,
Borne high upon thy clear-voiced accents, where
    Men mocked the Sign ;
Till that cold city heard thy battle-cry,
And hearts were stirred, and deemed a Pentecost
    was nigh.

Thou couldst a people raise, but couldst not rule :—
    So, gentle one,
Heaven broke at last the consecrated tool
    Whose work was done ;
According thee the lot thou lovedst best,
To muse upon times past,—to serve, yet be at rest,

                         δ.

XCVI.

BASIL.

BEAUTIFUL flowers round Wisdom's secret well,
   Deep holy thoughts of penitential lore,
   But dressed with images from Nature's store,
Handmaid of Piety. Like thine own cell
By Pontic mountain wilds and shaggy fell,
   Great Basil! there, within thy lonely door,
Watching and Fast and Prayer and Penance dwell,
   And sternly nursed Affections heavenward soar.
Without are setting suns and summer skies,
Ravine, rock, wood and fountain melodies;
And Earth and Heaven, holding communion sweet,
Teem with wild beauty. Such thy calm retreat,
Blest Saint! and of thyself an emblem meet,
All fair without, within all stern and wise.

                      ς.

XCVII.

THE AFRICAN CHURCH.

The gifts and calling of God are without repentance.

THE lions prowl around, thy grave to guard,
  And Moslem prayers profane
At morn and eve come sounding : yet unscar'd
  The Holy Shades remain :—
Cyprian, thy chief of watchmen, wise and bold,
  Trusting the lore of his own loyal heart,
And Cyprian's Master, as in age high-soul'd,
  Yet choosing as in youth the better part.
There, too, unwearied Austin, thy keen gaze
  On Atlas' steep, a thousand years and more,
Dwells, waiting for the first rekindling rays,
  When Truth upon the solitary shore
For the fall'n West may light his beacon as of yore.

γ.

XCVIII.

HOOKER.

" The night is far spent, the day is at hand."

VOICE of the wise of old !
Go breathe thy thrilling whispers now
In cells where learned eyes late vigils hold,
    And teach proud Science where to vail her brow.

Voice of the meekest man !
Now while the Church for combat arms,
Calmly do thou confirm her awful ban,
    Thy words to her be conquering, soothing
    charms.

Voice of the fearless Saint !
Ring like a trump, where gentle hearts
Beat high for truth, but, doubting, cower and faint ·—
    Tell them, the hour is come, and they must take
    their parts.

                         γ.

THE RULE OF FAITH.

XCIX.

Quod semper, quod ubique, quod ab omnibus.

1.

TRUTH through the Sacred Volume hidden lies
And spreads from end to end her secret wing,
Through ritual, type, and storied mysteries.
From this or that, when Error points her sting,
From all her holds, Truth's stern defences spring,
And Text to Text the full accordance bears,
Through every page the Universal King,
From Eden's loss unto the end of years,
From East unto the West, the Son of Man appears.

2.

Thus, when she made the Church her hallowed shrine
Founded on Jesus Christ the corner stone,
With Prophets and Apostles and the Line
Of ordered Ministers, Truth ever one,
Not here or there, but in the whole hath shone.
Whilst Heresies arise of varying clime
And varying form and colour, the true Sun,
One and the same through all advancing time,
The Whole His Mansion makes, vast, uniform, sublime

3.

Mark, how each Creed stands in that Test reveal'd,
Romish, and Swiss, and Lutheran novelties !
As in the light of Spenser's magic shield.*
Falsehood lets fall her poisoned cup and flies,
Rome's seven-headed monster sees and dies !
New forms of Schism which changing times supply,
Behold the unwonted light in wild surprise.
In darkness bold, bright-shining arms they spy,
And down their Parent's mouth the Imps of Error hie !

---

* The Faery Queen, B. i. c. viii. 21.   † B. i. c. i. 15.

4.

The Church her ample bosom may expand,
Again contract,—may open far and wide
Her tent, extend her cords, on either hand
Break forth, again into herself subside ;
Alike with her Faith's oracles abide,
Revered by fickle worshipper or spurn'd.
Oft faint, ne'er lost, the Lamp by Heaven supplied,
Oft dimm'd by envious mists, ne'er undiscern'd,
God's Witness, thro' all time, hath in His Temple burn'd.

5.

O Holy Truth, whene'er thy voice is heard,
A thousand echoes answer to the call ;
Tho' oft inaudible thy gentle word,
While we regard not.   Take me from the thrall
Of passionate Hopes, be thou my All in All ;
So may Obedience lead me by the hand
Into thine inner shrine and secret hall.
Thence hath thy voice gone forth o'er Sea and Land,
And all that voice may hear,—but none can understand,

6.

Save the obedient. From both love and hate,
Affections vile, low cares, and envy's blight,
And controversial leanings and debate,   .
Save me ! from earthly film my mental sight
Purge thou, make my whole body full of Light !
So may my eyes from all things Truth convey,
My ears in all thy lessons read aright,
My dull heart understand, and I obey,
Following where'er the Church hath mark'd t
    Ancient Way.

DISSENT.

C.

" That we should earnestly contend for the faith that was once
[for all] delivered unto the saints."—St Jude, 3.

ONE only Way to life :
One Faith, delivered once for all ;
One holy Band, endow'd with Heaven's high call;
One earnest, endless Strife ;—
This is the Church th' Eternal fram'd of old.

Smooth open ways, good store ;
A creed for every clime and age,
By Mammon's touch new moulded o'er and o'er ;
No cross, no war to wage ,
This is the Church our earth-dimm'd eyes behold.

N

But ways must have an end,
Creeds undergo the trial-flame,
Nor with th' impure the Saints for ever blend,
Heaven's glory with our shame —
Think on that hour, and choose 'twixt soft and bold

γ.

CI.

IDOLATRY AND DISSENT.

" The thing that hath been, it is that which shall be ; and th
which is done is that which shall be done , and there is no n
thing under the sun "

" THE thing that hath been, it shall be."
Through every clime and age
Doth haughty man, 'gainst Heav'n's decree,
The same mad warfare wage ;
Deeming, of old, the homage shame
Which One on High of right could claim,

Loathing a power that based not still
Its throne upon his own wild will,
Gods whom he chose, and made, he served alone,
And worshipped his own pride, in blocks of wood and
    stone.

" The thing that hath been, it shall be."
    The self-same pride this hour
Bids headstrong myriads round us flee
    The Church's sheltering bower.
Man, still unchanged, and still afraid
    Of power by human hands unmade,
    For all her Altar's rights divine,
    Will name his priest, will choose his shrine ;
And votaries, doomed in other days to bow
Within the idol's fane, throng the false prophet's now.

                a.

CII.

WHEN I would search the truths that in me burn,
And mould them into rule and argument,
A hundred reasoners cried ;—" Hast thou to learn
" Those dreams are scattered now, those fire
are spent ?"
And, did I mount to simpler thoughts and try
Some theme of peace, 'twas still the same reply.

Perplexed, I hoped my heart was pure of guile,
But judged me weak in wit, to disagree ;
But now I see, that men were mad awhile,
And joy the AGE TO COME will think with me ;
'Tis the old history ;—Truth without a home,
Despised and slain,—then, rising from the tomb.

ε.

CIII.

"I saw all Israel scattered upon the hills, as sheep that have not
a shepherd."

Poor wanderers, ye are sore distrest
To find that path which Christ has blest,
      Tracked by His saintly throng ;
Each claims to trust his own weak will,
Blind idol !—so ye languish still,
      All wranglers, and all wrong.

He saw of old, and met your need,
Granting you prophets of His creed,
      The throes of fear to suage ;
They fenced the rich bequest He made,
And sacred hands have safe conveyed
      Their charge from age to age.

Wanderers ! come home ! when erring most
Christ's Church aye kept the faith, nor lost
      One grain of Holy Truth .
She ne'er has erred as those ye trust,
And now shall lift her from the dust,
      And REIGN as in her youth !

δ.

RELIGIOUS STATES.

CIV.

PATRIARCHAL FAITH.

WE are not children of a guilty sire,
  Since Noe stepped from out his wave-tossed home,
  And a stern baptism flushed earth's faded bloom.
Not that the heavens then cleared, or cherub's fire
From Eden's portal did at once retire;
  But thoughts were stirred of Him who was to come,
  Whose rainbow hues so streaked the o'ershadowing
    gloom,
That faith could e'en that desolate scene admire.
The Lord has come and gone; and now we wait
The second substance of the deluge type,
When our slight ark shall cross a molten surge;
So, while the gross earth melts, for judgment ripe,
Ne'er with its haughty turrets to emerge,
We shall mount up to Eden's long lost gate.

δ.

CV.

HEATHENISM.

Mid Balak's magic fires
The Spirit spake clear as in Israel ;
With prayers untrue and covetous desires
    Did God vouchsafe to dwell ;
Who summoned dreams, His earlier word to bring
To holy Job's vexed friends, and Gerar's guileless
    king.

If such o'erflowing grace
From Aaron's vest e'en on the Sibyl ran,
Why should we fear the Son now lacks His place,
    Where roams unchristened man ?
As tho', when faith is keen, He cannot make
Bread of the very stones, or thirst with ashes slake.

                                                        δ.

CVI.

JUDAISM.

O piteous race!
Fearful to look upon ;
Once standing in high place,
Heaven's eldest son.
O aged blind
Unvenerable ! as thou flittest by,
I liken thee to him in pagan song,
In thy gaunt majesty,
The vagrant King, of haughty-purposed mind,
Whom prayer nor plague could bend ;*
Wronged, at the cost of him who did the wrong,
Accursed himself, but in his cursing strong,
And honoured in his end.

* Vide the Œdipus Coloneus of Sophocles.

O Abraham! sire
Shamed in thy progeny ;
Who to thy faith aspire,
Thy Hope deny.
Well wast thou given
From out the heathen an adopted heir,
Raised strangely from the dead, when sin had slain
Thy former-cherished care.
O holy men, ye first-wrought gems of heaven !
Polluted in your kin,
Come to our fonts, your lustre to regain !
O Holiest Lord ! . . . . but thou canst take no stain
Of blood, or taint of sin.

Twice in their day
Proffer of precious cost
Was made, Heaven's hand to stay
Ere all was lost.
The first prevail'd ;
Moses was outcast from the promised home
For his own sin, yet taken at his prayer
To change his people's doom.
Close on their eve, one other asked and failed ;

When fervent Paul was fain
The accursed tree, as CHRIST had borne, to bear,
No hopeful answer came,—a Price more rare
Already shed in vain.

δ.

CVII.

SUPERSTITION.

O LORD, and Christ, Thy Churches of the south
So shudder, when they see
The two-edged sword sharp-issuing from Thy mouth
As to fall back from Thee,
And seek to charms of man, or saints above,
To aid them against Thee, Thou Fount of grace an
love !

But I before Thine awful eyes will go
And firmly fix me there,
In my full shame ; not bent my doom to know,
Not fainting with despair ;
Not fearing less than they, but deeming sure,
If e'en Thy Name shall fail, nought my base heai
can cure.

δ.

CVIII.

SCHISM.

Oh, rail not at our brethren of the North,
  Albeit Samaria finds her likeness there ;
A self-formed Priesthood, and the Church cast forth
  To the chill mountain air.

What though their fathers sinned, and lost the grace
  Which seals the Holy Apostolic Line ?
Christ's love o'erflows the bounds His Prophets trace
  In His revealed design.

Israel had Seers ; to them the Word is nigh ;
  Shall not that Word run forth, and gladness give
To many a Shunamite, till in His eye
  The full Seven thousand live ?

                                                    δ.

CIX.

LIBERALISM

" Jehu destroyed Baal out of Israel   Howbeit from the sins
Jeroboam Jehu departed not from after them, to wit, the gold
calves that were in Bethel, and that were in Dan "

YE cannot halve the Gospel of God's grace ;

Men of presumptuous heart ! I know you well.

Ye are of those who plan that we should dwell,

Each in his tranquil home and holy place :

Seeing the Word refines all natures rude,

And tames the stirrings of the multitude.

And ye have caught some echoes of its lore,

As heralded amid the joyous choirs ;

Ye heard it speak of peace, chastised desires,

Good-will and mercy,—and ye heard no more ;

But, as for zeal and quick-eyed sanctity,

And the dread depths of grace, ye passed them by.

And so ye halve the Truth; for ye in heart,
  At best, are doubters whether it be true,
  The theme discarding, as unmeet for you,
Statesman or sages. O new-ventured art
Of the ancient Foe !—but what, if it extends
O'er our own camp, and rules amid our friends ?
                                δ.

CX.

APOSTASY

FRANCE ! I will think of thee, as what thou wast,
  When Poictiers showed her zeal for the true creed;
Or in that age, when holy truth, tho' cast
  On a rank soil, yet was a thriving seed
Thy schools within, from neighbour countries chased;
  E'en of thy pagan day I bear to read,
Thy Martyrs sanctified the guilty host,
The sons of blessed John, reared on a western coast

O

I dare not think of thee, as what thou art,
    Lest thoughts too deep for man should trouble me.
It is not safe to place the mind and heart
    On brink of evil, or its flames to see ;
Lest they should dizzy, or some taint impart,
    Or to our sin a fascination be.
And so by silence I will now proclaim
Hate of thy present self, and scarce will sound thy
    name.

                            δ.

CXI.

CONVERSION.

Once cast with men of language strange
    And foreign-moulded creed,
I marked their random converse change,
    And sacred themes succeed.

O how I coveted the gift
  To thread their mingled throng
Of sounds, then high my witness lift!
  But weakness chained my tongue.

Lord ! has our dearth of faith and prayer
  Lost us this power once given ;
Or is it sent at seasons rare,
  And then flits back to heaven ?

δ.

MOTHER AND CHILD.

CXII.

"When my father and my mother forsake me, the Lord taketh
me up."

MOTHER ! and hast thou left thy child
With winds unpitying in the wild,
Stretching his feeble arms from far,
Where coldly sets the Western Star ;*
    And is thy fostering bosom dry ?

My child ! upon me is a chain,
Mid those who have our Master slain ;
And signs I see of coming war,
Tempestuously it broods afar,—
    The night in silence driveth by.

* Canada.

Mother ! whate'er betide thee, save
The Robe and Arms He dying gave ;
That, thee to keep, a sheltering charm,—
And these thy foes, from their own harm ;
    O watch them wisely, warily !

My child ! I hold them still, but they
Would those immortal Arms essay,
And rend my sheltering Robe in twain ;
But aye with me shall they remain,—
    With them I live, with them I die !

Mother ! tis late with fear I cope,
And from my dangers gather hope :
The world grows sere, and I my bed
Have made of leaves around me shed,
    Till come the Day-spring from on high.

My Child ! whate'er shall me betide,
An Angel's face is at thy side ;
He, who amid the Arabian wild
Did with the mother save the child,
    Doth o'er thee lean, and hear thy cry.

Mother ! some Hand, through sky, o'er sea,
Leads wandering birds protectingly,
Mid floating piles, and ocean dark :
That Hand will guide thy homeless bark,
 Then leave them to their enmity.

My Child ! shall mine forsaken be,
That I may feed thy flock with thee ?
Yet know, ere they shall me bereave
Of my own Arms, yea, though I grieve,
 Unto thine icy hills I fly.

Mother ! our sun hath gone to rest,
But left behind a gleaming vest ;
It lies the western sky along,
And round me comes a starry throng,
 From out our Father's house on high.

My Child ! as darker grows the night,
Good Angels thus shall o'er thee light ;
And Memory, true to Him that's gone,
Shall take his torch and lead thee on,
 A moon unfelt, but calm and nigh.

ζ.

THE ANGEL OF THE CHURCH.

CXIII.

1.

Why is our glorious Angel seen to mourn,
　With earth-bent brow forlorn ?
Why hangs the cold tear on his cheeks ?
　Ah me ! his silence speaks ;
It is the Spoiler's parricidal hand,
　And the apostate land,
Which would herself God's candlestick displace,
　And put aside her cup of grace :
Hence, darkly gleaming through the nightly grove,
　　Bow'd down in pitying love,
　　Thou hearest all alone
　　The short precursive moan,
When in their mountain lair th' awakening thunders
　　move.

2.

" Not for the Spoiler's parricidal hand,
　　Nor the apostate land,
That I am darkly seen to mourn,
　　With earth-bent brow forlorn ;
But that the widowed Church, in hour of pride,
　　Her sackcloth laid aside,
Slumbering in Canaan's camp, and wakes to mou
　　Her ancient strength and glory shorn.
Where are thy weekly fasts ? Thy vigils where ?
　　　　Therefore each wandering air,
　　　　Comes o'er thee desolate ;
　　　　And ere it reach Heaven's gate,
Blows frustrate o'er the earth thy feeble-hearte
　　　　prayer."

3.

Tho flood-gates on me open wide,
　　And headlong rushes in the turbulent tide
Of lusts and heresies ! a motley troop they come
　　And old imperial Rome

Looks up and lifts again half-dead
  Her seven-horned head ;
And Schism and Superstition, near and far,
  Blend in one pestilent star,
And shake their horrid locks against the Saints to
  war.

4.

" Not for the flood-gates opening wide,
  I fear, nor for the turbulent rushing tide ;
But for the Church, so loth at her mysterious board
  To see her present Lord.
Therefore, around thine Altars deep,
  The Angels bow and weep ;
Or oh, in strength of Heaven's ennobling might,
  How should we see the light !
And one a thousand chase, ten thousand turn to
  flight !"

5.

Again I hear thy plaintive tale
  In the autumnal gale;
But, since thou passed'st through the fires,
  With our old martyr Sires,
Thou seem'st as one escaped the flame,
But looking back for something left behind;
The unshackled high resolve, the holier aim,
Single-eyed faith in loyalty resign'd,
  And heart-deep prayers of earlier years.
And, since that popular billow o'er thee past,
Which thine own Ken from out the vineyard cas
    Now, e'en far more
    Than then of yore,
An altered mien thy holy aspect wears.
  And oft thy half-averted brow
    Doth seem in act to go,
    With half out-spreading wings,
    And foot that heaven-ward springs;
Therefore to thee I draw, by fear made bold,
And strive with suppliant hand thy mantle skirts
    hold.

6.

" Can they who flock to Freedom's shrine,
  Themselves to me resign ?
There lift the Heav'n-defying brow,
  And here in meekness bow ?
 There to put on the soul aggrieved,
And attitude their high deserts to claim ,
Here kneel from their deserts to be relieved,
Claim nothing but the Cross, and their own shame?
  And now, behold and see
In holy place the ABOMINATION stands,
Whose breath hath desolated christian lands,
  In semblance fair,
  And saint-like air,
The Antichrist of heathen liberty !
 E'en on Religion's hallowed ground,
  He hath his altar found ;
  And now ere winter's net
  Is o'er thy pathway set,
 Haste and arise, to Judah's mountains flee
And drink the untainted fount of pure Antiquity."

       ζ.

LET US DEPART HENCE.*

CXIV.

Is there no sound about our Altars heard
   Of gliding forms that long have watched in vai
   For slumbering discipline to break her chain,
And aim the bolt by Theodosius feared?
"Let us depart;"—these English souls are scared,
   Who for one grasp of perishable gold,
   Would brave the curse by holy men of old
Laid on the robbers of the shrines they reared;

* Μεταβαίνωμεν ἐντευθεν. Among the portents which t‹
place before the taking of Jerusalem by the Romans, the follow
is mentioned by Josephus : " During the Festival which is cal
Pentecost, the Priests, by night, having come into the inner te
ple to perform their services, as was their custom, they repor
that they perceived, first a motion, a noise, and then they hear‹
it were a great crowd, saying, Let us depart hence." Vide Bis‹
Newton on the Prophecies, vol. ii. Dissert. 18·

Who shout for joy to see the ruffian band
Come to reform, where ne'er they came to pray,
E'en where, unbidden, Seraphs never trod.
Let us depart, and leave the apostate land
To meet the rising whirlwind as she may,
Without her guardian Angels and her God.

γ.

CXV.

(Athanasian Creed)

" SEEK we some realm where virgin souls may pray
 In faith untarnished by the sophist's scorn,
 And duly raise on each diviner morn
The Psalm that gathers in one glorious lay
All chants that e'er from heaven to earth found way :
 Majestic march ! as meet to guide and time
 Man's wandering path in life's ungenial clime,
As Aaron's trump for the dread Ark's array.
Creed of the Saints, and Anthem of the Blest,
And calm-breathed warning of the kindliest love
That ever heaved a wakeful mother's breast,
(True love is bold, and gravely dares reprove,)
Who knows but myriads owe their endless rest
To thy recalling, tempted else to rove ?

γ.

CXVI.

(Burial Service.)

" And they who grudge the Omnipotent His prais
What wonder if they grudge the dead his hope?
The irreverent restless eye finds room and scop
E'en by the grave, to wrangle, pry, and gaze.
Heaven in its mercy hides, but man displays;
   Heaven throws a gleam, where they would dark
     all;
A shade, where they, forgetting worm and pall,
Sing triumph; they excite, but Heaven allays.
Alas, for England's mourners, if denied
The soothing tones of Hope, though faint and low,
Or swoln up high, with partial tearless pride !
Better in silence hide their dead, and go,
Than sing a hopeless dirge, or coldly chide
The faith that owns release from earthly woe.

γ.

CXVII.

(Length of the Prayers)

" But Faith is cold, and wilful men are strong,
  And the blithe world, with bells and harness proud,
  Rides tinkling by, so musical and loud,
It drowns the Eternal Word, the Angelic Song ;
And one by one the weary listless throng
  Steals out of Church, and leaves the Choir unseen
  Of winged Guards to weep, where prayer had been,
That souls immortal find that hour too long.
Most fatal token of a falling age !
Wit ever busy, Learning ever new,
Unsleeping Fancy, Eloquence untired ;—
Prayer only dull ! The Saints' and Martyrs' page
A tedious scroll ; the scorned and faithful few
Left to bewail such beauty undesired."

γ.

CXVIII.

Sons of our Mother! such the indignant strain
  Might haply strike, this hour, a pastor's ear,
Purged to discern, for once, the aerial train
  Of heavenly Centinels yet lingering here;
  And what if, blending with the chant austere,
A soft inviting note attune the close?
  " We go ;—but faithful hearts will find us near,
Who cling beside their Mother in her woes,
Who love the Rites that erst their fathers loved,
Nor tire of David's Hymn, and JESUS' Prayer :—
Their quiet Altars, wheresoe'er removed,
Shall clear with incense sweet the unholy air ;
In persecution safe, in scorn approved,
Angels, and He who rules them, will be there.

                    γ.

CAPTIVITY.

CXIX.

"Many shall run to and fro, and knowledge shall be increased."

THERE is one only Bond in the wide earth
  Of lawful use to join the earth in one ;
  But in these weary times, the restless run
E'en to its distant verge, and so give birth
To other friendships, and joint-works to bind
Their hearts to the unclean whom there they find.
And so is cast upon the face of things
  A many webs to fetter down the Truth ;
  While the vexed Church, which gave in her fair
    youth
Prime pattern of the might which order brings,

But dimly signals to her distant seed,
There strongest found, where darkest in her creed.

O shame ! that Christian joins with Infidel
   In learned search and curious-seeming art !
   Burn we our books, if Christ's we be in heart,
Sooner than heaven should court the praise of hell!
Self-flattering age ! to whom shall I not seem
Pained with hot thoughts, the preacher of a dream :
                                     ẟ.

CXX.

> " I have a few things against thee, because thou sufferest th
> woman Jezebel, which calleth herself a prophetess, to teach an
> to seduce My servants to commit fornication, and to eat thin,
> sacrificed unto idols."

WEEP, Mother mine, and veil thine eyes with shame
    What was thy sin of old,
That men now give thy awful-sounding name
    To the false prophet's fold ?
    Whose flock thy crosier claim.

Sure thou hast practised in the tongues unclean
    Which Babel-masters teach ;
Slighting the Paraclete's true flame serene,
    The inimitative speech,
    Which throned thee the world's queen.

But, should earth-dust, from court or school of men,
    Have dimmed thy bridal gear,
When Wrath next walks his rounds, and in Heaven's
    ken
    Thy charge and works appear . . . . .
    Ah! thou must SUFFER then!

                           δ.

CXXI.

THE BEASTS OF EPHESUS.

" My soul is among lions : and I lie even among the children of
men, that are set on fire, whose teeth are spears and arrows, and
their tongue a sharp sword."

How long, O Lord of grace,
Must languish Thy true race,

In a forced friendship linked with Belial here ;
    With Mammon's brand of care,
    And Baal pleading fair,
And the dog-breed who at thy Temple jeer ?

    How long, O Lord, how long
    Shall Cæsar do us wrong,
Laid but as steps to throne his mortal power ?
    While e'en our Angels stand
    With helpless voice and hand,
Scorned by proud Haman, in his triumph-hour.

    'Tis said our seers discern
    The destined bickerings stern,
In the dim distance, of Thy fiery train.
    O nerve us in that woe !
    For, where Thy wheels shall go,
We must be tried, the while Thy foes are slain.

                  δ.

CXXII.

" I will give power unto My two witnesses, and they shall
prophesy."

How shall a child of God fulfil
His vow to cleanse his soul from ill,
And raise on high his baptism-light,
Like Aaron's seed in ritual white,
An holy-tempered Nazarite ?

First let him shun the haunts of vice,
Sin-feast, or heathen sacrifice;
Fearing the board of wealthy pride,
Or heretic, self-trusting guide,
Or where the adulterer's smiles preside.

Next, as he threads the maze of men,
Aye must he lift his witness, when
A sin is spoke in Heaven's dread face,
And none at hand of higher grace
The Cross to carry in his place.

But if he hears and sits him still,
First he will lose his hate of ill ;
Next, fear of sinning, after, hate ;
Small sins his heart then desecrate,
And last, despair persuades to great.

δ.

JEREMIAH.

CXXIII.

" Thou fallest away to the Chaldeans."

THEY say, " The man is false, and falls away :"
  Yet sighs my soul in secret for their pride ;
Tears are mine hourly food, and night and day
  I plead for them, and may not be denied.

They say, " His words unnerve the warrior's hand,
  And dim the statesman's eye, and disunite
The friends of Israel :" yet, in every land,
  My words, to Faith, are Peace, and Hope, and Might.

They say, " The frenzied one is fain to see
  Glooms of his own; and gathering storms afar ;—
But dungeons deep, and fetters strong have we."
  Alas ! heaven's lightning would ye chain and bar ?

Ye scorners of th' Eternal ! wait one hour ;
In His seer's weakness ye shall see His power.

γ.

CXXIV.

" I have set thee this day over the nations, and over the kingdon

" The Lord hath set me o'er the kings of earth,
　To fasten and uproot, to build and mar ;
　Not by mine own fond will : else never war
Had still'd in Anathoth the voice of mirth,
Nor from my native tribe swept bower and hearth
　Ne'er had the light of Judah's royal star
　Fail'd in mid heaven, nor trampling steed and c
Ceas'd from the courts that saw Josiah's birth.
'Tis not in me to give or take away,
But He who guides the thunder-peals on high,
He tunes my voice, the tones of His deep sway
Faintly to echo in the nether sky.
Therefore I bid earth's glories set or shine,
And it is so : my words are sacraments divine."

γ.

CXXV.

"This man is worthy to die for he hath prophesied against this city."

"No joy of mine to invite the thunder down,
  No pride, th' uprising whirlwind to survey,
How gradual from the north, with hideous frown,
  It veers in silence round th' horizon grey,
  And one by one sweeps the bright isles away,
Where fondly gaz'd the men of worldly peace,
  Dreaming fair weather would outlast their day.
Now the big storm-drops fall, their dream must cease—
They know it well, and fain their ire would wreak
  On the dread Arm that wields the bolt; but He
Is out of reach, therefore on me they turn;—
On me, that am but voice, fading and weak,
  A wither'd leaf inscrib'd with Heaven's decree,
And blown where haply some in fear may learn."

γ.

CXXVI.

" I said, I will not make mention of him… But his word was mine heart as a burning fire."

" SAD privilege is mine, to show
What hour, which way, the bitter streams will flow.
  Oft have I said, ' enough—no more
To uncharm'd ears th' unearthly strain I pour !'
  But the dread word its way would win,
Even as a burning fire my bones within,
  And I was forc'd to tell aloud
My tale of warning to the reckless proud."
    Awful warning ! yet in love
      Breath'd on each believing ear,
    How Heaven in wrath would seem to move
      The landmarks of a thousand year,
  And from the tablets of th' eternal sky
  The covenant oath erase of God most high.
  That hour, full timely was the leaf unrolled,
Which to the man belov'd the years of bondage tol
  And till his people's chain should be outworn,
Assigned him for his lot times past and times unbor

7

CXXVII.

"O ye remnant of Judah, go ye not into Egypt."

" O SWEETLY tim'd, as e'er was gentle hand
 Of mother prest on weeping infant's brow,
Is every sign that to His fallen land
 Th' Almighty sends by prophet mourners now.
 The glory from the ark is gone,—
 The mystic cuirass gleams no more,
 In answer from the Holy One,—
 Low lies the temple, wondrous store
Of mercies seal'd with blood each eve and morn;
Yet heaven hath tokens for faith's eye forlorn.

Heaven by my mouth was fain to stay
 The pride, that in our evil day,
Would fain have struggled in Chaldea's chain :
 Nay, kiss the rod; th' Avenger needs must reign :

And now, though every shrine is still,
Speaks out by me th' unchanging will :
‘ Seek not to Egypt ; there the curse will come ;
‘ But, till the woe be past, round Canaan roam,
‘ And meekly 'bide your hour beside your ruin'd
home.' ”

γ.

PROFANENESS.

CXXVIII.

AUTUMN

Now is the Autumn of the Tree of Life ;
   Its leaves are shed upon the unthankful earth,
Which lets them whirl, a prey to the winds' strife,
   Heartless to store them for the months of dearth.
   Men close the door, and dress the cheerful hearth,
Self-trusting still ; and in his comely gear,
Of precept and of rite, a household Baal rear.

But I will out amid the sleet, and view
   Each shrivelling stalk and silent-falling leaf ;
Truth after truth, of choicest scent and hue,
   Fades, and in fading stirs the Angel's grief,
   Unanswered here ; for she, once pattern chief
Of faith, my Country, now gross-hearted grown,
Waits but to burn the stem before her idol's throne.

δ.

CXXIX.

SAMUEL.

Thou chosen Judge of Israel's race,
　Grown grey in holy toil,
Whose lips are truth's own dwelling-place,
　Whose hands no bribe can soil,
And is it thus the tribes of God
Spurn thy meek rule and gifted rod?

Yet where are Dathan's cursed crew?
　And where Abiram's seed?
Must heaven its fires of wrath renew?
　Must earth repeat her deed,
And from the nations sweep away,
Who scorn the Prophet's gentle sway?

But no—the flames of holy zeal
　Sad pity's tears assuage;
Over his kindling eyes there steal
　Tears for God's heritage,
While for the rebel tribes flows forth
The prayer that stems Jehovah's wrath.

O Mother of our sinful land,
　By kings and saints of yore
Called to Britannia's savage strand
　From Syria's distant shore,
And do thy wayward children rage
'Gainst the meek sceptre of thine age?

And must each shrine of simple state,
　In purer days devote
To holy names yet consecrate,
　Where holy voices float,
In dust beneath their feet be trod
Who make the people's voice a god?

Then be it ;—of thy sons the while
　Be but the love more warm,
Nor their's to court the people's smile,
　Nor to the age conform.
So for our land their prayers may rise,
And God accept, when men despise.

CXXX.

Quiescere faciamus omnes dies festos Dei à terrâ.

WHEN first earth's rulers welcomed home
  The Church, their zeal impressed
Upon the seasons, as they come,
  The image of their guest.

Men's words and works, their hopes and fears,
  Henceforth forbid to rove,
Paused, when a Martyr claimed her tears,
  Or Saint inspired her love.

But craving wealth, and feverish power,
  Such service now discard ;
The loss of one excited hour
  A sacrifice too hard !

And e'en about the holiest day,
  God's own in every time,
They doubt and search, lest aught should stay
  The cataract of crime.

Where shall this cease ? must Crosiers fall,
  Shrines suffer touch profane,
Till, cast without His vineyard wall,
  The Heaven-sent Heir is slain?

CXXXI.

Christ's Church was holiest in her youthful days,
    Ere the world on her smiled ;
So now, an outcast, she would pour her rays
    More keen and undefiled ;
Yet would I not that hand of force were mine,
Which thrusts her from her awful ancient shrine.

'Twas duty bound each convert-king to rear
    His Mother from the dust,
And pious was it to enrich, nor fear
    Christ for the rest to trust ;
But who shall dare make common or unclean
What once has on the Holy Altar been ?

Dear Brothers !—hence, while ye for ill prepare,
    Triumph is still your own ;
Blest is a pilgrim Church !—Yet shrink to share
    The curse of breaking down.
So will we toil in our old place to stand,
Still calmly looking for the spoiler's hand.

                        δ.

CXXXII.

UZZAH AND OBED-EDOM.

Μὴ κίνει Καμαρίναν· ἀκίνητος γὰρ ἄμεινων.

THE ark of God has hidden strength,
　　Who reverence or profane,
They, or their seed, shall find at length,
　　The penalty or gain.

While as a sojourner it sought
　　Of old its destined place,
A blessing on the home it brought
　　Of one who did it grace.

But there was one, outstripping all
　　The holy-vestured band,
Who laid on it, to save its fall,
　　A rude corrective hand.

Read, who the Church would cleanse, and mark
　　How stern the warning runs ;
There are two ways to aid her ark,
　　As patrons and as sons.

δ.

CXXXIII.

ΠΕΡΙ ΤΗΣ ΜΙΣΗΤΟΥ ΣΤΑΣΕΩΣ.

" The Powers that be are ordained of God."

Yes, mark the words, deem not that saints alone
　　Are Heaven's true servants, and His laws fulfil
　　Who rules o'er just and wicked.　He from ill
Culls good, He moulds the Egyptian's heart of stone
To do him honour, and e'en Nero's* throne
　　Claims as His ordinance ; before Him still
　　Pride bows unconscious, and the rebel will
Most does His bidding, following most its own.
　　　Then grieve not at their high and palmy state,
Those proud bad men, whose unrelenting sway
Has shattered holiest things, and led astray
　　Christ's little ones : they are but tools of Fate,
　　Duped rebels, doomed to serve a Power they
　　　　hate,
To earn a traitor's guerdon, yet obey.

β.

* Rom. xiii. 1—8.

SACRILEGE.

CXXXIV.

" I have heard of Thee by the hearing of the ear, but now mine
eye seeth Thee " *Job* xlii. 5

1.

'TWAS on the day* when England's Church of yore
  Hail'd the New year—a day to angels known,
Since holy Gabriel to meek Mary bore
  The presence-token of th' Incarnate SON—
  Up a low vale a shepherd stray'd alone ;
Slow was his step and lowly bent his eye
  Save when at times a thought of tasks undone
IIis waken'd wincing memory stung too nigh :
Then startled into speed, else wandering.wearily.

* The above was written March 25, 1833, whilst the Irish Church
Bill was in progress.

2.

A Shepherd he, but not of lambs and ewes,
   But of that flock redeem'd with precious Blood ;
| Thoughtless too oft, now deeply seen to muse
    O'er the cold lea and by the rushing flood,
    And where the pathway skirts the leafless wood,
  And the heaped snow, in mockery of the spring,
    Lies mantling primrose flower and cowslip bud,
  And scared birds forget to build and sing,
So rudely the cold North has brush'd each tender wing.

3.

These Easter snows, of evil do they bode?
   Of Faith's fair blossoms withering ere their prime ;
And of a glorious Church that early glow'd
    Bright as yon Crown of Stars in cold clear time,
    That never sets, Pride of our arctic clime,
  Now deeply plung'd where tempests drive and sweep,
    Wavering and flickering, while rude guests of Crime
Rush here and there across th' ethereal deep,
And scarce one golden Isle her station seems to keep?

R

4.

Nay —'tis our human eyes, our airs of earth,
  That waver ; yet on high th' unquenched stars
Blaze as they blaz'd, and in their might go forth :
  The spouse of heaven nor crime nor rapine mars.
  But the MOST HIGH permits these earthly jars,
That souls yet hearing only, may awake
  And see him near, and feel and own the bars
'Twixt them and Him.   O be Thou near, to make
The worldly dream dissolve, the scared conscience
    ache !

5.

But chiefly theirs, who at Thine Altar serve,
  And for the souls elect Thy life-blood pour,
O grief and shame, when aged Pastors swerve
  To the base world or wild schismatic lore.
  Alas too lightly, by Thine open door,
They had been listening ; not within the shrine
  Kneeling in Christian calmness to adore,
Else had they held untir'd by Thee and Thine :
Nor gain nor fancy then had lur'd them from Thy
    shrine.

6.

Lord of a world in years, a Church decay'd,
  If from Thy whirlwind answering, as of old,
Thou with the vile wilt plead, till we have laid
    Our hand upon our mouth, and truly told
    Our tale of contrite Faith—(O not too bold
The prayer)—then welcome, whirlwind, anger, woe,
    Welcome the flash that wakes the slumbering fold
Th' Almighty Pastor's arm and eye to know,
And turn their dreamy talk to holy Fear's stern glow.

                                      γ.

CXXXV.

" But ye say, Wherein have we robbed Thee ? in tithes and
offerings. Ye are cursed with a curse: for ye have robbed Me,
even this whole nation."

HEARD ye? the unerring Judge is at the door !
  The curse of GOD is on thee, hapless Age,
  Binding thy brows with deadly sacrilege ;
Heaven's blight hath passed o'er thee! Talk no more :

Your talking must the rising sea outroar,
   Your schemes with God's own whirlwind must
       engage,
   Hand joined in hand with nature war must wage,
Your thoughts of good are toiling for a shore
Against the full Monsoon.   O teeming brood
Of hollow councils impotent to good !
O fullsailed bark ! God's Curse thy bearing wind,
And Sacrilege thy freight.   Strange pregnant scene,
While boldness mocks at judgment, and behind
Rises an Awful Form ! May I be clean !

                        ς.

JUDGMENT.

CXXXVI.

SIGHT AGAINST FAITH

"And Lot went out, and spake unto his sons-in-law, that married his daughters, and said, Up! get you out of this place, for the Lord will destroy this city. But he seemed as one that mocked unto his sons-in-law."

" Sunk not the sun behind yon dusky hill
Glorious as he was wont ? The starry sky
Spread o'er the earth in quiet majesty,
Discern'st thou in its clear deep aught of ill ?
Or in this lower world, so fair and still,
Its palaces and temples towering high ;
Or where old Jordan, gliding calmly by,
Pours o'er the misty plain his mantle chill ?
Dote not of fear, old man, where all is joy ;
And heaven and earth thy augury disown ;
And Time's eternal course rolls smoothly on,
Fraught with fresh blessings as day follows day.
The All-bounteous hath not given to take away;
The All-wise hath not created to destroy.

β.

CXXXVII.

PROSPERITY

" When they shall say, Peace and safety, then sudden destruction
cometh upon them '

WHEN mirth is full and free,
Some sudden gloom shall be ;
When haughty power mounts high,
The watcher's axe is nigh,
All growth has bound ; when greatèst found,
It hastes to die.

When the rich town, that long
Has lain its huts among,
Builds court and palace vast,
And vaunts,—it shall not last !
Bright tints that shine are but a sign
Of summer past.

And when thine eye surveys,
With fond adoring gaze,
And yearning heart, thy friend,—
Love to its grave doth tend.
All gifts below, save Truth, but grow
Towards an end.

δ.

CXXXVIII.

FAITH AGAINST SIGHT.

" As it was in the days of Lot, so shall it be also in the days of
the Son of man."

THE world has cycles in its course, when all
 That once has been, is acted o'er again :—
Not by some fated law, which need appal
 Our faith, or binds our deeds as with a chain ;
But by men's separate sins, which blended still
 The same bad round fulfil.

Then fear ye not, though Gallio's scorn ye see,
 And soft-clad nobles count you mad, true hearts !
These are the fig-tree's signs ; rough deeds must be,
 Trials and crimes ; so learn ye well your parts.
Once more to plough the earth it is decreed,
 And scatter wide the seed.

δ.

TRADE.

CXXXIX.

TYRE.

HIGH on the stately wall
    The spear of Arvad hung ,
Through corridor and hall
    Gemaddin's war-note rung.
Where are they now ? the note is o'er ;
Yes ! for a thousand years and more
Five fathom deep beneath the sea
Those halls have lain all silently ;
    Nought listing save the mermaid's song,
While rude sea-monsters roam the corridors along.

Far from the wandering East
    Tubal and Javan came,
And Araby the blest,
    And Kedar, mighty name.—
Now on that shore, a lonely guest,
Some dripping fisherman may rest,
Watching on rock or naked stone
His dark net spread before the sun,
Unconscious of the dooming lay,
That broods o'er that dull spot, and there shall brood
    for aye.

                      β.

CXL.

ENGLAND

TYRE of the West, and glorying in the name
    More than in Faith's pure fame!
O trust not crafty fort nor rock renowned
    Earned upon hostile ground;
Wielding Trade's master-keys, at thy proud will
To lock or loose its waters, England! trust not still.

Dread thine own power ' since haughty Babel's prime
    High towers have been man's crime.
Since her hoar age, when the huge moat lay bare,
    Strong holds have been man's snare.
Thy nest is in the crags ; ah ! refuge frail !
Mad counsel in its hour, or traitors will prevail.

He who scanned Sodom for His righteous men,
    Still spares thee for thy ten ;
But should vain hands defile the temple wall,
    More than His church will fall :
For, as Earth's kings welcome their spotless guest,
So gives He them by turn, to suffer or be blest.

                        δ.

CXLI.

UNITED STATES.

" Because that Tyrus hath said against Jerusalem, Aha ! she I
broken that was the gates of the people ; she is turned unto me
I shall be replenished, now she is laid waste : Therefore thus sait
the Lord God ; Behold, I am against thee, O Tyrus."

TYRE of the *farther* West ! be thou too warn'd,
    Whose eagle wings thine own green world o'erspread
Touching two Oceans : wherefore hast thou scorn'd
    Thy fathers' God, O proud and full of bread ?

Why lies the Cross unhonour'd on thy ground,
  While in mid air thy stars and arrows flaunt?
That sheaf of darts, will it not fall unbound,
  Except, disrob'd of thy vain earthly vaunt,
  Thou bring it to be bless'd where saints and
    Angels haunt?

The holy seed, by Heaven's peculiar grace,
  Is rooted here and there in thy dark woods;
But many a rank weed round it grows apace,
  And Mammon builds beside thy mighty floods,
Overtopping Nature, braving Nature's God;
  O while thou yet hast room, fair fruitful land,
Ere war and want have stain'd thy virgin sod,
  Mark thee a place on high, a glorious stand,
  Whence Truth her sign may make o'er forest, lake,
    and strand.

Eastward, this hour, perchance thou turn'st thine ear,
  Listening if haply with the surging sea,
Blend sounds of Ruin from a land once dear
  To thee and Heaven. O trying hour for thee!

Tyre mock'd when Salem fell · where now is Tyre?
  Heaven was against her. Nations thick as waves
Burst o'er her walls, to Ocean doom'd and fire :
  And now the tideless water idly laves
  Her towers, and lone sands heap her crowned
    merchants' graves.

7.

THE AGE.

CXLII.

THE RELIGION OF THE MAJORITY.

" TRUTH ! What is truth ? Shall Israel's king or state
Bow down, in Salem's costly shrine, to Him
Therein enthroned between the Cherubim,
Because the Lord is God? Nay, we but kneeled
Before the Ark, by yonder vail concealed,
Because that solemn Ark to consecrate
The people chose. Now, if that people's voice,
With altered tones, in idol hymns rejoice,
Lo ! we obey the mandate. Raise the cry—
Oh Baal, hear us ! To the host on high
Pour the drink-offering ! Moloch's burning throne,
Or Egypt's monsters, Israel's state shall own,
If Israel's tribes such deities demand.
Truth ! What is truth ? Shall Levi dare to brand

S

As false the creed the Gentile deems divine,
Or point to miracle, or mystic sign
Wrought, as he dreams, to prove the truth of yore?
Perish the thought: we heed such dreams no more;
Let Levi, let his brethren, learn that now
Kings to their people's gods—to them alone—will
    bow."

a.

CXLIII.

NATIONAL PROPERTY.

" Hark! Baal's praise resounds from countless choirs—
See gladdening nations hail his festal day—
While round the Lord's high shrine, the Levites' fires,
Some seven poor thousands, with Elijah, stay.
Then say, can they require, that scanty band,
Nay, can their puny sect presume to hold,
The wealth by monarchs erst, with lavish hand,
Down on Moriah's favoured altars told?
What kings have given, kings again may claim.
Then onward! To the Temple! In the name

Of David's line, of Judah's kingly throne,
Tear down th' inlaying gold of Solomon.
Nor view, ye timid few, our course with fear—
We reverence, reared, the shrine we would not rear,
And take not all.   With thankfulness receive
That portion of your own we deign to leave ;
And let the many, from your surplus store,
Mould their own idols.   We demand no more.
Speak ye of rights ? What right, in reason's eye,
Outweighs the sanction of a nation's nod ?
Who shall condemn a people ? Who deny
That people's privilege to choose their God ?"

a.

CXLIV.

NATIONAL DEGRADATION.

God of our Israel ! by our favoured sires
Once known, once honoured ! And is this the creed
Hailed, in their children's councils, with the meed
Of godless acclamation ; while the fires
Burn low on Thy dread Altar, and around
Th' advancing Gentile treads the hallowed ground ?

Yea, it is thus; and nerveless rulers hear,
Unholy triumph kindling in their eyes,
And catch fresh ardour from each maddening cheer
To urge the spoiler toward his glittering prize.
Yea, worst of all, not Bethel's priest alone,
Or Bel's adorer swells the plaudit's tone,
Thine own apostate worshipper, to Thee,
Mocking or self-deceived, who bends the knee,
Dares join the clamour, dares, though sworn to wait,
A faithful guard, before Thy vineyard's gate,
Tear down her fence, and bid the forest boar
Uproot Thy cherished vine on green Ierne's shore.

a.

CXLV.

PROSPECTS OF THE CHURCH.

AND where is now the Tishbite? Where is he
Should wave his master's robe, and call on Thee,
The Lord God of Elijah? All is o'er.
And while the Gentile scorns Thine awful frown,
Th' apostate digs Thy hallowed Altar down,
We see no sign, we hear no prophet more.

Nay, Bride of Heav'n! thou art not all bereft,
Though this world's prince against thy power rebels;
By thrones, dominions, wealth, and honours left,
Within thee still the ETERNAL SPIRIT dwells,
Thy pledged possession. Seek nor seer nor sign,
True Temple of that Habitant Divine;
Thy part is simple. Fearless still proclaim
The Truth to men who loathe her very name.
Proclaim that He, to Paul in glory shewn,
E'en from that glory, calls thy wrongs His own.
And if thy night be dark,—if tempests roll
Dread as the visions of thy boding soul,—
Still, in thy dimness, watch, and fast, and pray;
And wait the Bridegroom's call,—the burst of
    opening day.

                                                    a.

CHAMPIONS OF THE TRUTH.

CXLVI.

" Who shall go for us?" And I said, " Here am I : send me."

Dull thunders moan around the Temple Rock,
   And deep in hollow caves, far underneath,
The lonely watchman feels the sullen shock,
   His footsteps timing as the low winds breathe ;
Hark ! from the Shrine is asked, What steadfast heart
Dares in the storm go forth ? Who takes th' Almighty's
     part ?

And with a bold gleam flush'd, full many a brow
   Is raised to say, " Behold me, Lord, and send."
But ere the words be breath'd, some broken vow
   Remember'd, ties the tongue ; and sadly blend
With Faith's pure incense, clouds of conscience dim,
And faltering tones of guilt mar the Confessor's hymn.

                          γ.

CXLVII.

THE CREED

IF waiting by the time-crown'd halls,
Which nurtur'd us for CHRIST in youth,
  We love to watch on the grey walls
The lingering gleam of Evangelic Truth;—
  If to the spoilers of the soul,
  Proudly we shew our banner'd scroll,
  And bid them our old war-cry hear,
  " GOD IS MY LIGHT :* whom need I fear !"
How bleak, that hour, across our purpose high,
Sweeps the chill damping shade of thoughtless years
      gone by !

  How count we then lost eve and morn,
The bell unwelcom'd, prayer unsaid,
  And holy hours and days outworn
In youth's wild race, Sin's lesson newly read !

---

* " Deus illuminatio mea," is the motto of the University of
Oxford.

Then deem we, "ill could Angels brook
The lore that on our lips we took,
On lips profane celestial lore :"
And hardly dare we keep the door,
Though sentries sworn : the memory thrills so keer
How with unready hearts at first we ventur'd in.

γ.

CXLVIII.

SPOLIATION.

But sadder strains, and direr bodings dark,
Come haunting round th' Almighty's captive ark,
By proud Philistian hosts beset,
With axe and dagger newly whet
To hew the holy gold away,
And seize their portion as they may.
Fain would we fix th' unswerving foot, and bare
The strong right arm, to share
The glorious holy war ; but how undo
The knot our Fathers tied? Are we not spoilers too

How for God's altar may that arm be bold,
Where cleaves the rust of sacrilege of old ?
    Oh, would my country once believe,
    But once her contrite bosom heave,
    And but in wish or vow restore
    But one fair shrine despoil'd of yore !
How would the windows of th' approving sky
      Shower down the dews on high !
Arm'd Levites then, within the Temple dome,
Might we the foe await, nor yet profane God's home.

Vain, disappointing dream ! but oh ! not vain,
  If haply on the wakening heart remain
    The vow of pure self-sacrifice,
    The conscience yearning to devise
    How God may have His treasure lost,
    And we not serve Him without cost.
  To such methought, I heard an Angel say,
      " Offer not all to-day,
While spoilers keep the shrine : yet offer all,
Treasurer of God's high cause. half priestly is thy
    call."

                     γ.

CXLIX.

CHURCH AND KING.

Nor wants there Seraph warnings, morn and eve,
 And oft as to the holiest Shrine we bear
 Our pure, unbloody gifts, what time our prayer
In Heaven's sure ward all Christian Kings would leave.
Why should that prayer be faltering? Wherefore heave
 With sadness loyal hearts, when hallow'd air
 That solemn suffrage hears? Alas! our care
Is not for storms without, but stains that cleave
 Ingrain'd in memory, wandering thoughts profane;
Or worse, proud thoughts of our instructress meek,
 The duteous Church, heaven-prompted to that
  strain.
Thus, when high mercy for our King we seek,
 Back on our wincing hearts our prayers are
  blown
 By our own sins, worst foes to England's throne.

And with our own, the offences of our land
　　Too well agree to build our burthen high,
　　Christ's charter blurr'd with coarse, usurping
　　　　hand,
And gall'd with yoke of feudal tyranny
The shoulders where the keys of David lie.
　　Angel of England ! who might thee withstand ?
Who for the spoil'd and trampled Church deny
　　Thy suit in Heaven's high courts, might one
　　　　true band
　　Of holy brethren, breathing English air,
　　Be found, their Cross in thine array to bear,
And for their Mother cast Earth's dreams away ?
　　Till then, all gaily as our pennons glance,
　　And at the trumpet's call the brave heart dance.
In fear and grief for Church and King we pray.

　　　　　　　　　　　　　　　7.

CL.

OXFORD

(From Bagley, at 8 A. M *)*

THE flood is round thee, but thy towers as yet
 Are safe, and clear as by a summer's sea
 Pierce the calm morning mist, serene and free,
To point in silence heavenward. There are met
Thy foster-children;—there in order set
 Their nursing fathers, sworn to Heaven and Thee
 (An oath renewed this hour on bended knee,)
Ne'er to betray their Mother nor forget.—
Lo! on the top of each aerial spire
What seems a star by day, so high and bright,
It quivers from afar in golden light:
But 'tis a form of earth, though touched with fire
Celestial, raised in other days to tell
How, when they tired of prayer, Apostles fell.

γ.

FIRE.

PART I.

"The Lord thy God is a consuming fire "

CLI.

NADAB AND ABIHU.

" Away, or ere the Lord break forth !
  The pure ethereal air
Cannot abide the spark of earth,
  'Twill lighten and not spare."

" Nay, but we know our call divine,
  We feel our hearts sincere ;
What boots it where we light our shrine,
  If bright it blaze and clear."

T

God of the unconsuming fire,
  On Horeb seen of old,
Stay, Jealous One, Thy burning ire . . . .
  It may not be controlled !

The Lord breaks out, the unworthy die ;
  Lo ! on the cedar floor
The robed and mitred corses lie—
  Be silent and adore.

Yet sure a holy seed were they,
  Pure hands had o'er them past,
Cuirass and crown, their bright array,
  In Heaven's high mould were cast.

Th' atoning blood had drench'd them o'er,
  The mystic balm had seal'd ;
And may the blood atone no more,
  No charm the anointing yield ?

Silence, ye brethren of the dead,
  Ye Father's tears, be still :
But choose them out a lonely bed,
  Beside the mountain rill ;

Then bear them as they lie, their brows
    Scath'd with the avenging fire,
And wearing (sign of broken vows)
    The blest, the dread attire.

Nor leave unwept their desert grave,
    But mourn their pride and thine,
Oft as rebellious thought shall crave
    To question words divine.

                    γ.

CLII.
THE BURNING AT TABERAH

THE fire of Heaven breaks forth,
When haughty Reason pries too near,
  Weighing th' eternal mandate's worth
  In philosophic scales of earth,
Selecting these for scorn, and those for holy fear.

Nor burns it only then ·
The poor that are not poor in heart,—
  Who say, " The bread of Christian men,
  We loathe it, o'er and o'er again,"—
The murmurers in the camp, must feel the blazing dart.

Far from the Lord's tent door,
And therefore bold to sin, are they :
" What should we know of Faith's high lore!"
Oh! plead not so—there's wrath in store,
And temper'd to our crimes the lightnings find thei
 way.

        ᵞ.

CLIII.

KORAH. DATHAN AND ABIRAM.

Dathan and Abiram

" How long endure this priestly scorn,
Ye sons of Israel's eldest born?
Shall two, the meanest of their tribe,
To the Lord's host the way prescribe,
And feed our wildering phantasy
With every soothing dream and lie
Their craft can coin? We see our woe,
Lost Egypt's plenty well we know :
But where the milk and honey?—where
The promised fields and vineyards fair?

Lo ! wise of heart and keen of sight
Are these—ye cannot blind them quite—
Not as our sires are we : we fear not open light."

Korah.

"And we too, Levites though we be,
We love the song of liberty.
Did we not hear the Mountain Voice
Proclaim the Lord's impartial choice ?
The camp is holy, great and small,
Levites and Danites, one and all ;
Our God His home in all will make.—
What if no priestly finger strake
Or blood or oil o'er robe or brow,
Will He not hear His people's vow ?
Lord of all Earth, will he no sign
Grant but to Aaron's haughty line ?
Our censers are as yours : we dare you to the shrine."

Thus spake the proud at prime of morn ;
Where was their place at eve ? Ye know,
Rocks of the wild in sunder torn,
And altars scath'd with fires of woe !

Earth heard and sank, and they were gone;
Only their dismal parting groan
   The shuddering ear long time will haunt.
Thus rebels fare: but ye profane,
Who dar'd th' anointing power disdain
   For freedom's rude unpriestly vaunt,
Dire is the fame for you in store:
Your molten censers evermore
. Th' atoning altar must inlay;
Memorial to the kneeling quires
That Mercy's God hath judgment-fires
   For high-voic'd Korahs in their day.

                       γ.

CLIV.

ELIJAH AND THE MESSENGERS OF AHAZIAH

On! surely Scorner is his name,
Who to the Church will errands bring
From a proud world or impious king,
   And, without fear or shame,
In mockery own them "men of God,"
O'er whom he gaily shakes the miscreant spoiler's rod.

But if we be God's own indeed,
Then is there fire in Heaven, be sure,
And bolts deep-wounding, without cure,
 For the blasphemer's seed ;—
Wing'd are they all, and aimed on high,
Against the hour when Christ shall hear His martyrs'
 cry.

Oh ! tell me not of royal hosts ;—
One hermit, strong in fast and prayer,
Shall gird his sackcloth on, and scare
 Whate'er the vain earth boasts :
And thunder-stricken chiefs return
To tell their Lord how dire the Church's lightnings
 burn

γ.

FIRE.

PART II

" Our God is a consuming fire "

CLV.

THE SAMARITANS SPARED.

AND dare ye deem God's ire must cease
    In Christ's new realm of peace?
'Tis true, beside the scorner's gate
The Lord long-suffering deign'd to wait,
    Nor on the guilty town
Call'd the stern fires of old Elijah down
    A victim, not a judge, He came,
With His own blood to slake th' avenging flame.

Now, by those hands so rudely rent
    The bow of Heaven is bent;
And ever and anon His darts
Find out even here the faithless hearts,
    Now gliding silently,
Now rushing loud, and blazing broad and high,
    A shower or ere that final storm
Leave earth a molten ocean without form.

True Love, all gentle though she be,
    ·Hath eyes, the wrath to see :
Nor may she fail in faith to pray
For hastening of Redemption's day,
    Though with the triumph come
Forebodings of the dread unchanging doom :—
    Though with the Saints' pure lambent light
Fires of more lurid hue mysteriously unite.

                      γ.

CLVI.

JULIAN

DREAD glimpses, even in gospel times, have been ,
Nor was the holy Household mute,
Nor did she not th' Avenger's march salute
With somewhat of exulting mien.—
Angel harps ! of you full well
That measure stern
The Church might learn
When th' apostate Cæsar fell ;—
Proud Champion he, and wise beyond the rest,
His shafts not at the Church, but at her Lord addrest.

What will He do, the Anointed One on high,
Now that hell-powers and powers of Rome
Are branded to reverse His foemen's doom,
And mar His Sovereign Majesty ?
Seers in Paradise enshrin'd !
Your glories now
Must quail and bow
To th' high-reaching force of mind—

Vainly o'er Salem rolls your dooming tone
Her sons have heard, this hour, a mightier trumpet
blown.

The foes of Christ are gathering, sworn to build
　Where He had sworn to waste and mar ;
　Plummet and line, arms of old Babel's war,
　　Are ready round Moriah's field.—
　　　But the clouds that lightning breathe
　　　　Were ready too, ·
　　　　And, bursting through,
　　　Billows from the wrath beneath
　　For Christ and for His Seers so keenly wrought,
They half subdu'd to faith the proud man's dying
thought

γ·

CLVII.

THE FALL OF BABYLON.

But louder yet the heavens shall ring,
And brighter gleam each Seraph's wing,

When doom'd of old by every Prophet's lyre,
　Theme of the Saints' appealing cry,
　While underneath the shrine they lie,
Proud Babel in her hour sinks in her sea of fire.

　While worldlings from afar bemoan
　The shatter'd Antichristian throne,
The golden idol bruis'd to summer dust—
　" Where are her gems ?—her spices, where ?
　Tower, dome, and arch, so proud and fair—
Confusion is their name—the name of all earth's
　　trust."

　The while for joy and victory
　Seers and Apostles sing on high,
Chief the bright pair who rest in Roman earth ·
　Fall'n Babel well their lays may earn,
　Whose triumph is when souls return,
Who o'er relenting Pride take part in Angels' mirth.

CLVIII.

THUS evermore the Saints' avenging God
  With His dread fires hath scath'd th' unholy ground;
Nor wants there, waiting round th' uplifted rod,
  Watchers in heaven and earth, aye faithful found.

God's armies, open-ey'd, His aim attend,
  Wondering how oft these warning notes will peal,
Ere the great trump be blown, the Judge descend :
  Man only wears cold look and heart of steel.

Age after age, where Antichrist hath reign'd
  Some flame-tipt arrow of th' Almighty falls,
Imperial cities lie in heaps profan'd,
  Fire blazes round apostate council-halls.

And if the world sin on, yet here and there
  Some proud soul cowers, some scorner learns to
        pray ;
Some slumberer rouses at the beacon glare,
  And trims his waning lamp, and waits for day.

THE EXCHANGE.

CLIX.

"The grass withereth, the flower fadeth, but the Word of our
God shall stand for ever."

'Tis sad to watch Time's desolating hand
   Doom noblest things to premature decay;
   The Feudal court, the Patriarchal sway
Of kings, the cheerful homage of a land
Unskill'd in treason, every social band
    That taught to rule with sweetness, and obey
    With dignity, swept one by one away;
While proud Empirics rule in fell command.
Yet, Christian! faint not at the sickening sight;
Nor vainly strive with that supreme Decree.
Thou hast a treasure and an armoury
Locked to the spoiler yet: Thy shafts are bright:
Faint not: HEAVEN'S KEYS are more than sceptred
     might;
Their Guardians more than king or sire to thee.

β

CXL.

"Instead of thy fathers thou shalt have children, whom thou
mayest make princes in all lands."

SAY, who is he, in deserts seen,
　Or at the twilight hour ?
Of garb austere, and dauntless mien,
Measured in speech, in purpose keen,
Calm, as in heaven he had been,
　Yet blithe when perils lower.

My holy Mother made reply,
　"Dear Child, it is my Priest.
The world has cast me forth, and I
Dwell with wild earth and gusty sky ;
He bears to men my mandates high,
　And works my sage behest.

Another day, dear Child, and thou
　Shalt join his sacred band.
Ah ! well I deem, thou shrinkest now
From urgent rule and severing vow ;
Gay hopes flit round, and light thy brow :—
　Time hath a taming hand !"

δ.

COMMUNE PONTIFICUM.

"At even, being the first day of the week, the doors were shut where the disciples were assembled for fear of the jews."

CLXI

" Are the gates sure ?—is every bolt made fast ?
  No dangerous whisper wandering through—
Dare we breathe calm, and, unalarmed, forecast
  Our calls to suffer or to do ?"
O ye of little faith ! twelve hours ago,
  He whom ye mourn, by power unbound
The bonds ye fear ; nor sealed stone below
  Barred Him, nor mailed guards around.

The Lord is risen indeed ! His own have seen,
    They who denied, have seen His face,
Weeping and spared.   Shall loyal hearts not lean
    Upon his outstretched arm of grace ?
Shine in your orbs, ye stars of GOD's new Heaven,
    Or gathered or apart, shine clear !
Far, far beneath the opposing mists are driven,
    The Invisible is waiting near.

γ.

"JESUS CAME, AND STOOD IN THE MIDST, AND SAITH
UNTO THEM, PEACE BE UNTO YOU.   AND WHEN HE
HAD SO SAID, HE SHOWED THEM HIS HANDS AND HIS
SIDE.   THEN WERE THE DISCIPLES GLAD WHEN THEY
SAW THE LORD."

CLXII.

Is He not near ?—look up and see :
Peace on His lips, and in His hands and side
The wounds of love, He stays the trembling knee,
    Nerves the frail arm, His ark to guide.

Is He not near ? O trust His seal
Baptismal, yet uncancelled on thy brow ;
Trust the kind love His holy months reveal,
Oft as His altar hears thy deep heart-searching vow.

And trust the calm, the joy benign,
That o'er the obedient breathes in life's still hour,
When Sunday-lights with summer airs combine,
And shadows blend from cloud and bower.
And trust the wrath of JESUS' foes ;
They feel Him near, and hate His mark on you ;
O take their word, ye whom He loved and chose !
Be joyful in your King , the rebels own you true.

γ.

" THEN SAID JESUS UNTO THEM AGAIN, PEACE BE UNTO
YOU AS MY FATHER HATH SENT ME, SO SEND I YOU."

CLXIII.

AND shrink ye still ?—He nearer draws,
And to His mission and His cause

Welcomes His own with words of grace and might:
"Peace be to you!"—their peace, who stand
In sentry with GOD's sword in hand,
The peace of CHRIST's loved champions warring in
His sight.

"Peace be to you!"—their peace, who feel
E'en as the SON the FATHER's seal,
So they the SON's; each in his several sphere
Gliding on fearless Angel wing,
One heart in all, one hope, one KING,
Each an Apostle true, a crowned and robed seer.

Sent as the FATHER sent the SON,
'Tis not for you to swerve nor shun
Or power or peril; ye must go before:
If caught in the fierce bloody shower,
Think on your LORD's o'erwhelming hour;
Are ye not priests to Him who the world's forfeit
bore?

Throned in His church till He return,
Why should ye fear to judge and spurn*
This evil world, chained at his feet and yours ?
Why with dejected faltering air
Your rod of more than empire bear ?
Your brows are royal yet; GOD's unction aye endures.

γ.

" AND HAVING SAID THIS, HE BREATHED ON THEM, AND
SAITH UNTO THEM, RECEIVE YE THE HOLY GHOST."

CLXIV.

BY your Lord's creative breath,
Breathing Hope and scorn of death ;
Love untired, on Pardon leaning,
Joy, all mercies sweetly gleaning ;
Zeal, the bolts of Heaven to dart,
Fragrant Purity of heart ;—
By the voice ineffable,
Wakening your mazed thoughts with an Almighty
spell ;

* Vide Rev. ii. 26—28, which is also addressed to a Christian
bishop

By His word, and by His hour
When the PROMISE came with power,—
By His HOLY SPIRIT's token,
By His saintly chain unbroken,
Lengthening, while the world lasts on,
From His cross unto His throne,—
Guardians of His Virgin Spouse !
Know　that　His　might　is　yours,　whose　breathing
　　sealed your vows.

γ.

" WHOSESOEVER SINS YE REMIT, THEY ARE REMITTED
UNTO THEM; AND WHOSESOEVER SINS YE RETAIN,
THEY ARE RETAINED."

CLXV.

BEHOLD your armoury !—sword and lightning shaft,
　Culled from the stores of God's all-judging ire,
And in your wielding left ! The words, that waft
　Power to your voice absolving, point with fire

Your awful curse.　O grief! should Heaven's
　　dread Sire
Have stayed, for you, the mercy-dews of old
　　Vouchsafed, when pastors' arms in deep desire
Were spread on high to bless the kneeling fold!
IF CENSURE SLEEP, WILL ABSOLUTION HOLD?

Will the great KING affirm their acts of grace
Who careless leave to cankering rust and mould
　　The flaming sword that should the unworthy chase
From His pure Eden? O beware! lest vain
Their sentence to *remit*, who never dare *retain*.

7.

PATIENCE.

CLXVI.

THE AFFLICTED CHURCH.

τλῆθι, λέων, ἄτλητα παθών, τετληότι θυμῷ

BIDE thou thy time !
Watch with meek eyes the race of pride and crime,
Sit in the gate, and be the heathen's jest,
    Smiling and self-possest.
O thou, to whom is pledged a victor's sway,
    Bide thou the victor's day !

    Think on the sin
That reaped the unripe seed, and toiled to win
Foul history-marks at Bethel and at Dan,
    No blessing, but a ban ;

Whilst the wise Shepherd* hid his heaven-told fate,
    Nor recked a tyrant's hate.

    Such need is gain ;
Wait the bright Advent that shall loose thy chain !
E'en now the shadows break, and gleams divine
    Edge the dim distant line.
When thrones are trembling, and earth's fat ones
      quail,
    True Seed ! thou shalt prevail !

                          δ.

CLXVII.

THE BACKWARD CHURCH

" Can a woman forget her sucking child, that she should no
have compassion on the son of her womb ? Yea, they may forget
yet will I not forget thee "

WAKE, Mother dear, the foes are near,
    A spoiler claims thy child ;
This the sole refuge of my fear,
    Thy bosom undefiled.

              * David.

What spells of power, in this strange hour,
  My Mother's heart enslave ?
Where is thy early bridal dower,
  To suffer and to save ?

Thee then I sue, Sleepless and True,
  Dread Maker reconciled !
Help ere they smite, Thy shrine in view,
  The Mother with the child.

δ.

CLXVIII.

THE GATHERING OF THE CHURCH.

" He which hath begun a good work in you, will perform it
    until the day of Jesus Christ."

WHEREFORE shrink, and say, " 'Tis vain ;
In their hour hell-powers must reign ;
Vainly, vainly would we force
Fatal Error's torrent course ;
Earth is mighty, we are frail,
Faith is gone, and Hope must fail."

x

Yet along the Church's sky
Stars are scattered, pure and high;
Yet her wasted gardens bear
Autumn violets, sweet and rare—
Relics of a spring-time clear,
Earnests of a bright new year.

Israel yet hath thousands sealed,
Who to Baal never kneeled;
Seize the banner, spread its fold!
Seize it with no faltering hold!
Spread its foldings high and fair,
Let all see the Cross is there!

What, if to the trumpet's sound
Voices few come answering round?
Scarce a votary swell the burst,
When the anthem peals at first?
GoD hath sown, and He will reap;
Growth is slow when roots are deep;

HE will aid the work begun,
For the love of His dear SON;
HE will breathe in their true breath,
Who serene in prayer and faith,
Would our dying embers fan
Bright as when their glow began.

γ.

CLXIX.

THE CHURCH IN PRAYER.

" Thou meetest him that rejoiceth and worketh righteousness,
those that remember Thee in Thy ways."

WHY loiterest within Simon's walls,
  Hard by the barren sea,
Thou Saint! when many a sinner calls
  To preach and set him free?

Can this be he, who erst confessed
  For CHRIST affection keen,
Now truant in untimely rest,
  The mood of an Essene?

Yet he who at the sixth hour sought
   The lone house-top to pray,
There gained a sight beyond his thought,—
   The dawn of Gentile day.

Then reckon not, when perils lower,
   The time of prayer mis-spent;
Nor meanest chance, nor place, nor hour,
   Without its heavenward bent.

                         δ

CLXX.

THE CHURCH IN BONDAGE

Remember my bonds

O COMRADE bold of toil and pain!
   Thy trial how severe,
When severed first by prisoner's chain
   From thy loved labour-sphere.

Say, did impatience first impel
   The heaven-sent bond to break?
Or couldst thou bear its hindrance well,
   Loitering for Jesu's sake?

O might we know ! for sore we feel
  The languor of delay,
When sickness lets our fainter zeal,
  Or foes block up our way.

Lord ! who Thy thousand years dost wait
  To work the thousandth part
Of Thy vast plan, for us create
  With zeal a patient heart !

$\delta.$

CLXXI.

THE PROSPECTS OF THE CHURCH.

" And He said, It is finished "

CHRIST only, of GOD's messengers to man,
Finished the work of grace, which He began ;
E'en Moses wearied upon Nebo's height,
  Though loth to leave the fight
With the doomed foe, and yield the sun-bright land
  To Joshua's armed hand.

And David wrought in turn a strenuous part,
Zeal for GOD's house consuming him in heart ,
And yet he might not build, but only bring
        Gifts for the heavenly King,
And these another reared, his peaceful Son,
        Till the full work was done.

List, Christian warrior ! thou, whose soul is fain
To rid thy Mother of her present chain ;—
CHRIST will unloose His Church ; yea, even now
        Begins the work, and thou
Shalt spend in it thy strength ; but, ere He save,
        Thy lot shall be the grave.

                                    δ.

DISAPPOINTMENT.

CLXXII.

ROME

FAR sadder musing on the traveller falls
 At sight of thee, O Rome !
Than when he views the rough sea-beaten walls
 Of Greece, thought's early home ;
For thou wast of the hateful Four, whose doom
 Burdens the Prophet's scroll ;
But Greece was clean, till in her history's gloom
 Her name and sword a Macedonian stole.

And next a mingled throng besets the breast
 Of bitter thoughts and sweet ;
How shall I name thee, Light of the wide West,
 Or heinous error-seat ?
O Mother erst, close tracing Jesus' feet !
 Do not thy titles glow
In those stern judgment-fires, which shall complete
 Earth's strife with Heaven, and ope the eternal woe ?

δ.

CLXXIII.

THE CRUEL CHURCH.

O Mother Church of Rome ! why has thy heart
   Beat so untruly towards thy northern child ?
   Why give a gift, nor give it undefiled,
Drugging the blessing with a step-dame's art ?
Why bare thy sword ? beneath thy censure's smart
   Long days we writhed, who would not be beguiled ;
   While thy keen breath, like blast of winter wild,
Froze, till it crumbled, each sublimer part
Of rite or work, devotion's flower and prime.
Thus have we lain, thy charge, a dreary time,
Christ's little ones, torn from faith's ancient home,
To dogs a prey. And now thou sendest foes,
Bred from thy womb, lost Church ! to mock the throes
Of thy free child, thou cruel-natured Rome !

                        δ.

CLXXIV.

THE GOOD SAMARITAN

O THAT thy creed were sound !
For thou dost soothe the heart, Thou Church of Rome,
  By thy unwearied watch and varied round
Of service, in thy Saviour's holy home.
  I cannot walk the city's sultry streets,
  But the wide porch invites to still retreats,
Where passion's thirst is calmed, and care's unthank-
    ful gloom.

    There on a foreign shore
The homesick solitary finds a friend .
  Thoughts, prisoned long for lack of speech, outpour
Their tears ; and doubts in resignation end.
  I almost fainted from the long delay,
  That tangles me within this languid bay,
When comes a foe, my wounds with oil and wine to
    tend.

                       c.

CLXXV.

When I am sad, I say,
  " What boots it me to strive,
And vex my spirit day by day
  Dead memories to revive ?

Alas ! what good will come,
  Though we our prayer obtain,
To bring old times triumphant home,
  And Heaven's lost sword regain ?

Would not our history run
  In the same weary round,
And service, in meek faith begun,
  One time in forms be bound ?

Union would give us strength,—
  That strength the earth subdue ;
And then comes wealth, and pride at length,
  And sloth, and prayers untrue."

Nay, this is worldly-wise ;
  To reason is a crime,
Since the LORD bade His Church arise,
  In the dark ancient time.

He wills that she should shine ;
  So we her flame must trim
Around His soul-converting Sign,
  And leave the rest to him.

                                                       δ.

CLXXVI.

MOSES SEEING THE LAND

MY Father's hope ! my childhood's dream !
  The promise from on high !
Long waited for ! its glories beam
  Now when my death is nigh.

My death is come, but not decay ;
  Nor eye nor mind is dim ;
The keenness of youth's vigorous day
  Thrills in each nerve and limb.

Blest scene ! thrice welcome after toil—
   If no deceit I view ;
O might my lips but press the soil,
   And prove the vision true !

Its glorious heights, its wealthy plains,
   Its many-tinted groves,
They call ! but He my steps restrains
   Who chastens whom He loves

Ah ! now they melt . . . . they are but shades . . .
   I die !—yet is no rest,
O Lord ! in store, since Canaan fades
   But seen, and not possest ?

                                        δ.

WAITING FOR CHRIST

CLXXVII.

ISRAEL.

" And all his sons and all his daughters rose up to comfort him,
but he refused to be comforted."

O SPECIOUS sin and Satan's subtle snare,
   That urges sore each gentlest meekest heart,
   When its kind thoughts are crushed and its wounds
     smart,
World-sick to turn within and image there
Some idol dream, to lull the throbbing care !
   So felt reft Israel, when he fain would part
   With living friends, and called on memory's art
   To raise the dead and soothe him by despair.
Nor err they not, although that image be
God's own, nor to the dead their thoughts be given,—
Earth-hating sure, but yet of earth enthralled ;
For who dare sit at home, and wait to see
High Heaven descend, when man from self is called
Up through this thwarting outward world to Heaven ?

                        δ.

CLXXVIII.

Do not their souls, who 'neath the Altar wait
    Until their second-birth,
The gift of patience need, as separate
    From their first friends of earth ?
Not that earth's blessings are not all outshone
    By Eden's Angel flame,
But that earth knows not yet, the Dead has won
    That crown, which was his aim.
For when he left it, 'twas a twilight scene
    About his silent bier,
A breathless struggle, faith and sight between,
    And Hope and sacred Fear.
Fear startled at his pains and dreary end,
    Hope raised her chalice high,
And the twin-sisters still his shade attend,
    Viewed in the mourner's eye.

So day by day for him from earth ascends,
    As dew in summer-even,
The speechless intercession of his friends,
    Toward the azure heaven
Ah! dearest, with a word he could dispel
    All questioning, and raise
Our hearts to rapture, whispering all was well,
    And turning prayer to praise.
And other secrets too he could declare,
    By patterns all divine,
His earthly creed retouching here and there,
    And deepening every line.
Dearest! he longs to speak, as I to know,
    And yet we both refrain:
It were not good; a little doubt below,
    And all will soon be plain.

                        $\delta.$

CLXXIX.

THE NEW JERUSALEM.*

" And I saw the Holy City, new Jerusalem, coming down from God out of heaven, prepared as a Bride adorned for her Husband "

THE Holy Jerusalem
From highest heaven descending,
And crowned with a diadem
Of Angel bands attending,
The Living City built on high,
Bright with celestial jewelry!

She comes, the Bride, from heaven gate,
In nuptial new Adorning,
To meet the Immaculate,
Like coming of the morning.
Her streets of purest gold are made,
Her walls a diamond palisade.

(* *From the Paris Breviary, in Festo Dedicationis*)

There with pearls the gates are dight
Upon that Holy Mountain;
    And thither come both day and night,
    Who in the Living Fountain
Have washed their robes from earthly stain,
And borne below Christ's lowly chain.

    By the hand of the Unknown
    The Living Stones are moulded
        To a glorious Shrine, ALL ONE,
    Full soon to be unfolded;
The building wherein God doth dwell,
The Holy Church Invisible.

    Glory be to God, who layed
    In heaven the foundation;
        And to the Spirit who hath made
    The walls of our salvation;
To Christ himself the Corner Stone,
Be glory! to the Three in One.

THE END.

INDEX.

INDEX.

INDEX.

INDEX

INDEX.

INDEX.

INDEX

Henry Mozley and Sons, Printers, Derby

BIBLIOLIFE

Old Books Deserve a New Life
www.bibliolife.com

Did you know that you can get most of our titles in our trademark **EasyScript**™ print format? **EasyScript**™ provides readers with a larger than average typeface, for a reading experience that's easier on the eyes.

Did you know that we have an ever-growing collection of books in many languages?

Order online:
www.bibliolife.com/store

Or to exclusively browse our **EasyScript**™ collection:
www.bibliogrande.com

At BiblioLife, we aim to make knowledge more accessible by making thousands of titles available to you – quickly and affordably.

Contact us:
BiblioLife
PO Box 21206
Charleston, SC 29413

Printed in Great Britain by
Amazon.co.uk, Ltd.,
Marston Gate.